SYMBOLIZING THE PAST

Reading *Sankofa, Daughters of the Dust,* *& Eve's Bayou* as Histories

Sandra M. Grayson

University Press of America, ® Inc.
Lanham • New York • Oxford

Copyright © 2000 by
University Press of America, ® Inc.
4720 Boston Way
Lanham, Maryland 20706

12 Hid's Copse Rd.
Cumnor Hill, Oxford OX2 9JJ

Library of Congress Cataloging-in-Publication Data

Grayson, Sandra M.
Symbolizing the past : reading Sankofa, Daughters of the dust, & Eve's bayou
as histories / Sandra M. Grayson.
p. cm.
1.   Afro-Americans in motion pictures. I. Title.
PN1995.9.N4 G73   2000   791.43'6520396073—dc21   00-039224 CIP

ISBN 0-7618-1727-1 (pbk: alk. ppr.)

⊖™ The paper used in this publication meets the minimum
requirements of American National Standard for Information
Sciences—Permanence of Paper for Printed Library Materials,
ANSI Z39.48—1984

To Jimmie R. Grayson, Jr. (my husband)

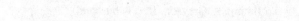

Contents

Foreword

Dr. Sandra M. Grayson's book *Symbolizing the Past: Reading Sankofa, Daughters of the Dust, and Eve's Bayou as Histories* derives from her scholarly interest in African American Studies and in the hope that the exegeses of works included will be helpful to critics, to researchers, to students, and to the general reader.

One main purpose is to assist scholars in identifying African American works that are considered of paramount importance and to examine their images and meanings—appreciative, interpretive, descriptive, normative, textual, and genetic. Films are evaluated that best express the African American mind and African American spirit.

Dr. Grayson's book analyzes Black films with attention to theme, cultural construction, characterization, moral-philosophical implications, Black images, and historical context to Black life and conditions. A good critic writes candidly about the alienation and protest against the surrounding majority, gives us analyses of powerful African American literary, historical, sociological, and biographical works, and presents us the "flavor" of racial identity, experience, and heritage. Dr. Grayson's masterpiece of criticism is rooted in our past and reminds us that we should keep African American works alive. In so doing, we keep African American Studies alive, challenging, and energetic.

Finally, the beauty of this book is Dr. Grayson's command of the English language and her ability to write with an almost poetic prose style.   Good critics show a propensity for balance—phrase with phrase or clause with clause—and give their prose a definite rhythm. *Symbolizing the Past* is packed with thought, eloquence, and intellectual interest.   The prose is powerful in its hard realism and lyrically beautiful in its description.

This book compels us to assume greater individual social responsibility and to work toward transcendence.

Leonard A. Slade, Jr.
National President
The Langston Hughes Society and
Professor of Africana Studies and English
University of Albany, State University of New York
March 2000

Preface

Through a selection of images, *Sankofa, Daughters of the Dust*, and *Eve's Bayou* create an intricate tapestry of the past. Although the films are fictional, they are infused with factual information and grounded in historical research. The linkages between the iconography in the works and experiences of enslaved Africans and their descendants in North America are central to the films. Unburdened by a linear progressive construct of history, the works utilize the visual and symbolic, as well as community-based narratives, to represent many of the historical realities of slavery. As political texts, they serve to redefine Black history and mythic memory in an effort to decolonize minds. *Symbolizing the Past* extends the study of *Sankofa, Daughters of the Dust*, and *Eve's Bayou* into a broader conceptual framework by analyzing the films within African and African American cultural and historical contexts. This interdisciplinary approach integrates the theoretical and the grassroots by examining archival materials, primary and secondary texts, and fieldwork in order to decode the signs in the films.

Chapter 1

Images Past/Signs Transformed

One night during slavery, the owls walked like a group of men to the sand-bar in Congaree Swamp in South Carolina. After the other animals arrived, the owls held court. Brer Buzzard stood accused. The morning after the customary sitting up all night with the deceased (Brer Rabbit's brother) and his family, Brer Rabbit and the other animals had to go to work. Brer Buzzard (who was an undertaker) was supposed to bury Brer Rabbit's brother, but Brer Buzzard ate him. The jay-bird accused Brer Buzzard. When Brer Rabbit and the other animals sought justice, the owls formed the court, and Brer Buzzard was found guilty. The owl and jay-bird are usually associated with evil, dread, and death in African American oral narratives, details which indicate that Brer Buzzard's crime in the folktale "The Animal Court" is more heinous than any actions of the owl or jay-bird. Although Brer Buzzard did not kill Brer Rabbit's brother (he was already physically dead), his crime was that he did not perform the proper burial based on traditional West African practices. Hence, Brer Buzzard's actions may have permanently harmed Brer Rabbit's brother's spirit and caused his spirit to wander endlessly.

In "The Animal Court," Brer Rabbit is connected to religion in that he arranged for his brother to receive a proper burial then sought justice after his brother was not properly buried. In a similar vein, Brer Rabbit is associated with religion in the folktale "Bur Rabbit in

Red Hill Churchyard." In that tale, Brer Rabbit is a religious leader in an African ceremony. He used the power of his fiddle to call up the dead ancestor (Simon), allow the living and the dead to communicate, and make the entire scene disappear:

> Brer Rabbit is shown as a man of God [in "Bur Rabbit in Red Hill Churchyard"], and new possibilities are opened for understanding him as a figure in Afro-American folklore heretofore unappreciated for religious functions.[1] (Stuckey 18-20)

Embedded in "The Animal Court," "Bur Rabbit in Red Hill Churchyard," and other Black folktales are traditional West African beliefs. Enslaved Africans in antebellum North America preserved and passed on African history/memory and culture primarily through oral narratives. The high art of the oral tradition continues in contemporary African American communities, as well as through a growing number of films, a medium that for many Black filmmakers has served as an extension of the African American oral tradition. During the 1990s, for example, several films grounded in African American history were produced, directed, and/or written by people of African descent.[2] *Symbolizing the Past* focuses on three of these films--*Sankofa*, *Daughters of the Dust*, and *Eve's Bayou*--and is an analysis of the ways in which the films image African American history. Similar to African American oral narratives, the films are multi-faceted, revealing much through the spoken word but even more through symbols. When juxtaposed, they function as a continuous narrative about enslaved Africans and their descendants in North America, vignettes that represent experiences spanning from the antebellum period through the 20th century. While the events in *Sankofa* are firmly grounded in the antebellum period and *Daughters of the Dust* is set in 1902 frequently flashing back to the slave era, *Eve's Bayou* segues into the present as an adult Eve recalls the family events that transpired when she was ten years old. These narratives are non-linear moving in and through time and linking the past (one of slavery in North America) to the present.

Although *Sankofa*, *Daughters of the Dust*, and *Eve's Bayou* are fictional narratives in which factual information is infused with an imaginative construction creating a mythic memory, the creative artists attempted to accurately represent experiences of enslaved Africans and their descendants in North America, and the films are grounded in historical research. Haile Gerima, for example, spent 20 years researching, writing, and producing *Sankofa*. Julie Dash completed extensive research on Gullah culture and had a historical advisor (Dr. Margaret Washington Creel, an expert on Gullah) on the project. Dash wanted to bring "a basic integrity to the historical events" (Baker 164). In addition to her own historical research, Kasi Lemmons "consulted experts in Creole culture and relied on the knowledge of cast members who were reared in the area" for her film *Eve's Bayou* (Brown 39).

Symbolizing the Past extends the study of *Sankofa, Daughters of the Dust*, and *Eve's Bayou* into a broader conceptual framework by analyzing the films within African and African American cultural and historical contexts. This interdisciplinary approach integrates the theoretical and the grassroots by examining archival materials, primary and secondary texts, and fieldwork in order to decode the signs within the films. Since these films are grounded in the historical reality of slavery, it is important to concentrate, initially, on the slave community in North America and the oral tradition, subjects on which the next chapter focuses.

Notes

[1]Furthermore, Brer Rabbit is the "keeper of the faith of the ancestors, mediator of their claims on the living, and supreme master of the forms of creativity" (Stuckey 18-20).

[2]These films include *Daughters of the Dust* (Julie Dash 1991), *Malcolm X* (Spike Lee 1992), *Sankofa* (Haile Gerima 1993), *Rosewood* (John Singleton 1996), *Eve's Bayou* (Kasi Lemmons 1997), and *Beloved* (Oprah Winfrey 1998, based on Toni Morrison's novel).

Chapter 2

History, Memory, & the African American Oral Tradition

During the antebellum period in North America, the historical prophets of enslaved African communities preserved and passed on African history/memory and culture primarily through oral narratives. Frederick Douglass described the slave community as a circle that he was within as a slave, a community that relied on codes for survival, escape,[1] and resistance (a technique I refer to as the "encoding strategy"). Primarily because of the laws which prohibited slaves from practicing African religions and because they were taught through early discipline never to say anything uncomplimentary about their masters, enslaved Africans encoded their thoughts, beliefs, and traditions in songs, animal tales, and oral narratives so as to be unrecognizable to the master. This body of knowledge remained private (that is, information of which the master was not aware).

Meetings and gatherings away from whites were cornerstones of the private lives of enslaved Africans. When "stealing the meeting" (having a secret meeting), enslaved Africans would often drag a bush in back of them, to obliterate their footprints so that the pater-rollers[2] would not catch them without a pass (Hurmence *Before Freedom* 69). In order to secure the area as much as possible, someone would watch for pater-rollers and warn the slaves of any danger.[3] Simon Brown, a former slave in Virginia, remembered being a lookout for a prayer meeting during which the sermon reflected some of the private thoughts of the enslaved. After Brown heard pater-rollers approaching and warned the slaves, the preacher's message instantly became a public one intended for the white pater-rollers to report to the slave master. When the pater-rollers were gone, the preacher continued the private sermon (Faulkner 30-31).

Secret societies were another private element of the slave community. In Virginia's cities, for example,

> societies to take care of the sick and provide acceptable funerals existed [. . .]. Most of these societies were secret. They had secretaries who kept records with numbered codes. Members would drift in, state their numbers, and make payment without telling their names. Societies usually had a "privileged" slave as president. This slave could move freely and so keep in current communication with members. In the case of a funeral, members of the Richmond society surreptitiously sat together during the service. Afterwards, once they were far enough away from white surveillance, they formed a column of march. The conference reported that members reputedly "were faithful to each other and . . . every obligation was faithfully carried out." The system had developed to this rather complex stage by the early nineteenth century. (Kuyk 561)

Secret meetings and careful planning were also crucial to organizing revolts.[4] Probably the largest slave revolt in American history started in present-day LaPlace on Andry's Woodland Plantation in Louisiana on January 8, 1811 and continued past the River Road plantations gathering support along the way down to present-day Kenner; this revolt involved at least 500 slaves. Among the numerous other slave revolts in North America were the Stono Uprising in South Carolina (1739) led by an enslaved African named Jemmy[5] and Madison Washington's successful revolt on the slave ship *Creole* (1841). The *Creole* was carrying 135 slaves from Virginia to a slave market in New Orleans. After Washington took control of the ship, he had the crew sail to Nassau where the slaves were given asylum then freed.[6]

Although it was against the law for slaves to teach each other to read and write, enslaved Africans often organized secret schools and meetings for this purpose. For instance, Milla Granson and Frederick Douglass, while slaves, created secret schools to teach other slaves. Granson ran a secret midnight school in which hundreds of slaves learned to read and write. Many of these slaves wrote passes and escaped to Canada. Douglass began a Sabbath school for slaves around 1834. He held classes at the house of a free Black man. The students and the teacher knew that if they were caught the minimum punishment was thirty-nine lashes. In a similar vein, Harriet Jacobs arranged meetings to teach a fellow slave to read. She recalled when Uncle Fred asked her to teach him to read, "He thought he could plan to come three times a week without its being suspected. I selected a quiet nook, where no intruder was likely to penetrate" and taught him to read (Jacobs 72).

Through songs, enslaved Africans expressed their protests, spiritual beliefs, as well as codes for escape and secret messages to other slaves. For example, the following spiritual provided details about an escape (I included the meaning of the code in brackets):

> This train [*group of escapees*] is bound for
> glory [*freedom*], this train
> This train is bound for glory, this train,
> This train is bound for glory,
> Get on board [*prepare to leave*] and tell your story [*when you reach freedom, tell the story of your life in slavery, escape, and freedom so that the information could be recorded and used in the anti-slavery movement*]
> This train is bound for glory, this train.
> This train don' t pull no extras [*no extra escapees*], this train,
> This train don't pull no extras, this train,
> This train don' t pull no extras,
> Don't pull nothing but the midnight special [*escapees leaving at midnight*],
> This train don't pull no extras, this train. (Goode 89)

When Frederick Douglass and several other slaves were planning escape, the following song was their favorite:

> I thought I heard them say,
> There were lions in the way,
> I don't expect to stay
> Much longer here
> Run to Jesus--shun the danger
> I don't expect to stay
> Much longer here. (*My Bondage and My Freedom* 278)

This song had multiple meanings. "In the lips of some, it meant the expectation of a speedy summons to a world of spirits; but in the lips of our company, it simply meant a speedy pilgrimage toward a free state, and deliverance from all the evils and dangers of slavery"

(Douglass, *My Bondage and My Freedom* 278-279). Similarly, the message of escape was part of the following spiritual:

> Let us break bread together on our knees.
> Let us break bread together on our knees.
> We will fall on our knees and
> We will face the rising sun
> Oh, Lord have mercy if you please.

In the documentary *When Animals Talked*, William J. Faulkner explained that this song was an attack on the institution of slavery and meant that Harriet Tubman was going to meet a group of slaves in the morning at a prearranged location facing the east. Tubman would then lead the slaves to freedom. Harriet Tubman, the most successful leader of the Underground Railroad, escaped from slavery then returned to the South 19 times and led over 300 slaves (including her family) to freedom. Tubman asserted, "There was one of two things I has a *right* to, liberty, or death, if I could not have one, I would have de oder, for no man should take me alive; I should fight for my liberty as long as my strength lasted" (29).

In addition to the message of escape, some spirituals such as "Follow the Drinking Gourd" contained links to West African traditions. The title of the song refers to "the path that one can take to the North by following the Big Dipper" (Goode 90). The spiritual says in part:

> When the sun comes back and the first quail calls,
> Follow the drinking gourd,
> For the old man is a-waiting for to carry you to freedom,
> Follow the drinking gourd. (Goode 90)

"The text mirrors the West African tradition of fashioning eating and drinking utensils out of gourds" (Goode 90). Enslaved African families had a well from which they drew water on a southern plantation. The water was left in a bucket on a table where family members and friends "could take a drink using a dipper that was carved out of a gourd. The gourd or dipper was also used as a symbol of freedom; it was hung over the doorways of stations along the Underground Railroad" (Goode 90).

Similar to the spirituals, African American oral narratives contained meanings intended for those who were inside the circle of the slave community. Ralph Ellison noted that African American oral narratives tell what life was really like for Blacks in North America; he looked for what the narratives say and do not say which is extremely important given the subtlety of meaning in the oral narratives. In addition, these narratives often provide insights into traditional West African belief systems. In the case of the following discussion, that belief system is Ifa as projected in "The King Buzzard," "Transmigration," and "The Yellow Crane," three folktales in *Tales of the Congaree*, a collection of Black folktales from South Carolina compiled by E. C. L. Adams.

Bird Imagery, Ifa, & African American Oral Narratives[7]

One of the unspoken issues within some of the animal tales in *Tales of the Congaree* is the link between the animal imagery and the real experiences of Blacks in the United States, especially in South Carolina. Another unexplained level of these tales is the West African influences within them. "The King Buzzard," for example, reflects the Igbo belief that "the spirit of the deceased returns to this world in the form of an animal if, before death, the deceased 'murdered' one or more human beings" (Stuckey 6). Furthermore, the punishment depicted in the "The King Buzzard" (the eternal wandering of the soul)

> probably discouraged members of the slave community from collaborating with their slave masters [. . . and this tale] almost certainly helped enhance spiritual and political unity in slave communities in which the tale was told. (Stuckey 6)

The Ifa influence (which is revealed through bird images) is yet another dimension of the tales. In the following sections, I analyze the Ifa influence in "The King Buzzard," "Transmigration," and "The Yellow Crane." The Ifa worldview (or *world sense*, for not all cultures rely primarily on sight to understand the world) projected in these tales through the Ifa concepts of self-in-the-universe and reincarnation reflect some of the private beliefs of the enslaved Africans.

"The King Buzzard" & "Transmigration:"
A Summary

In "The King Buzzard," Tad, the central person in both tales, told his friends that he was walking along Big Alligator Hole in Congaree Swamp when he saw an enormous buzzard with red eyes. Tom, who listened to Tad's account, explained that what Tad saw was not a buzzard; it was the spirit of an African chief who betrayed his people. Tom's father told him that during slavery an African chief helped whites trap thousands of Africans on slave ships. One day the whites took the chief to America as a slave. When the chief died, the *Great Master* decided to punish him by making him wander for eternity in the form of a buzzard.

"Transmigration" focuses on Tad's interaction with an owl sitting on a tree limb. The owl was the spirit of Ole Man Smart Daniel's Daddy, a friend of Tad's grandfather and a former slave. The owl/spirit revealed that he lived inappropriately in this world. After Tad looked closely at the owl, he realized that the owl was a person who looked extremely old and wicked. As Tad escaped, the spirit floated behind him laughing and hollering. Eventually, Tad safely returned to the camp where his friends were gathered.

For comparative purposes, I also highlight in this section an *ese* Ifa (poem of Ifa) about Agbigbo[8] (an Ifa priest who became a bird that carries a "load of evil" on its head and is a symbol of unfaithfulness in Ifa priests). Although no *ese* Ifa is identical to "The King Buzzard" or "Transmigration," there are significant parallels in the use of bird imagery between the following poem of Ifa and the South Carolinian narratives.

The very first divination practice of Orunmila's[9] children after they had been initiated as Ifa priests was to present Orunmila with all of the money they had made on their journey. Orunmila would then keep one-tenth of the money and give the rest to each child. Agbigbo was among the children referred to although he was actually the child of Orunmila's wife and another man with whom she had an affair during Orunmila's sixteen years absence. Even though Agbigbo was not Orunmila's blood child, Orunmila taught Agbigbo the secrets of divination and sent him on a tour of distant lands to perform divination. Upon his return, Agbigbo buried his gain of twenty thousand cowries at the city gate and told Orunmila that he had made no profit. Later, Agbigbo went back to the gate:

> He dug out the twenty thousand cowries which he buried there,

Placed it on his head,
And went towards Ikoolo,
His father's city [. . .[10]].
As soon as Agbigbo placed the twenty thousand cowries on the
head,
Esu [[11]] pointed his small medicine gourd at him,
And the load of money got stuck to his head,
And became a piece of iron. (Abimbola, *Sixteen Great Poems of
Ifa* 224-226)

Esu then turned into wind, went to the city of Ikoolo, and
warned the people that one of their sons was returning, but he
carried a "load of evil" on his head. Hence, the people should
not allow him to put down the load. "If you allow him to do so,"
warned Esu, "your homes would be smashed, your ways would
be smashed" (Abimbola, *Sixteen Great Poems of Ifa* 228).
When Agbigbo arrived at Ikoolo, the people blocked the road
and shouted, "It is death that you are carrying into this land. We
will not share in it. Agbigbo-niwonran take away your load.
Take away your evil load. [. . .] It is disease which you are
bringing into this city" (Abimbola, *Sixteen Great Poems of Ifa*
228).[12]   As a result of Esu's actions,

> Agbigbo was turned away from his father's city and in shame and
> disgrace, he entered into the forest and became a bird carrying
> about the "load of evil" on his head. That "load of evil" is
> represented by the pad in the middle of that bird's head. In Ifa
> divination poetry, the Agbigbo bird is usually regarded as a fake
> Ifa priest who deceives and cheats his own clients. Furthermore,
> he is believed to be in league with the evil supernatural powers
> known collectively as ajogun [. . .]. (Abimbola, *Sixteen Great
> Poems of Ifa* 210)

There are significant parallels in the use of bird imagery in this *ese*
Ifa about Agbigbo and the two tales from South Carolina. In all three
narratives, for example, the birds were originally people who
committed a negative deed, and as part of their punishment they were
reincarnated (or turned) into certain types of birds.   These birds
symbolize the negative deed for which the individuals were punished
and serve as a warning to other people who might contemplate
committing the same action. The birds in each narrative also critique
the real life situation in which the individual was involved. A parallel
can also be drawn between the special characteristics of the birds in

the narratives and the particular human characteristics of the individuals who represent the birds. For instance, Agbigbo carried a load of evil on his head, and the Agbigbo bird has a tuft in the middle of its head. The birds in the narratives function as projections of human action.

Ifa: An Overview

Ifa is a system of belief with a complex literary corpus divided into 256 distinct *Odu* (categories); each *Odu* has 600 *ese* (poems/verses). The literary corpus has numerous branches of knowledge categorized as follows:

> Ogeere--general knowledge of Ifa literature including memorization of hundreds of ese in each Odu;
> Odu to te ilu--literature telling histories and myths about the foundation of particular Yoruba towns and villages;
> Aasan--literature dealing with magic, incantations, and healing by the power of words;
> Iwosan--healing by herbal prescriptions accompanied by the making of the appropriate sacrifices; and
> Iyere--chanting of Ifa. (Abimbola, "Ifa as a Body of Knowledge" 1)[13]

Merchants and priests spread Ifa from the city of Ife in Yorubaland before the 15th century through much of the Lower Guinea cultural zone (modern-day Ivory Coast, Togo, Benin, Nigeria, Ghana, and Cameroon). Ife was an important city to a large portion of people:

> From the various oral traditions, it seems clear that it was at Ife that the institutions of kingship and centralized kingdom first emerged in Yorubaland through the conquest and unification of some of the existing communities and states in the area by a dynasty founded by the semi-legendary figure of Oduduwa. (Boahen 63)

Ife (the center of the highly developed works of art in bronze, ivory, wood, and terra cotta) "probably dates back to the Nok culture (1000 BC - 200 AD) and was where the method of using bronze in sculpture by the *cire perdue* (or "lost wax") process was probably first developed," a process that spread from Ife into the Benin Kingdom, as well as throughout West Africa (Boahen 64).

The elite and religious experts of the Lower Guinea cultural zone knew the details of Ifa. The general public was familiar with the basic values and ideas within it.[14] Ifa was well established in a good part of the Lower Guinea cultural zone particularly where the Oyo Empire (present-day Togo, Benin, and Western Nigeria) was dominant. It is clear that Ifa spread from the city of Ife before the 15th century through the Lower Guinea cultural zone in Atlantic Africa.[15] By the mid-17th century, Ifa could be found in the neighboring Kingdom of Ardra in modern Benin (Dahomey).[16] By the end of the 17th century, Ifa was found on both the Gold Coast (modern-day Ghana) and the Ivory Coast. Early written reports of Ifa divination were recorded by Bosman who was on the Gold Coast and Slave Coast during the 1690s as a trading agent of the Dutch West Indies Company, although the English translation of his book was published in 1705. Another early account was from Assinie in the Ivory Coast by Loyer in 1714.

Numerous enslaved Africans in South Carolina from the Lower Guinea cultural zone[17] came out of the Ifa tradition. I hypothesize that by 1807 enslaved Africans in South Carolina from the Lower Guinea cultural zone had established and created aspects of "The King Buzzard," "Transmigration," and "The Yellow Crane."

Ifa Concepts of Self-in-the-Universe & Reincarnation in "The King Buzzard" & "Transmigration"

Among important concepts expressed in the Ifa literary corpus is the self-in-the-universe. "The term 'self-in-the-universe' has been coined to convey the joint connotation of two Yoruba expressions: *wiwalaaye* (just being alive) and *wiwalaye* (being alive, healthy, and pursuing socially desirable attainments)" (Morakinyo 76). The three major areas which comprise the self-in-the-universe are the individual's self, psychosocial environment, and the religio-metaphysical sphere of her/his life. These three areas are essential to understand the motivational aspects of human behavior in the Ifa tradition. The self is made up of two parts, the *ori* (also called *ayanmo*--that which has been selected as part of oneself) and the *eni*. The *ori* constitutes the unconscious part of the self since it is unknown to the individual. The *eni* is the conscious self that is aware of the nature of manifested behavior and is responsible for ensuring the well being of the individual. (Morakinyo 74-76)

An analysis of behavior involves a total person as a self-in-the-universe when incorporating an understanding of the various interactions among the self, psychosocial environment, and religio-spiritual sphere (taking place during any moment in any individual). In accord with these dynamics, the buzzard in "The King Buzzard" and the owl in "Transmigration" function as malevolent elements of the psychosocial environment interacting with the conscious self and belong in the category of evil supernatural powers. In Ifa, the *ajogun*[18] (malevolent supernatural powers) work against humans by trying to prevent the timely achievement of people's destiny.

In "The King Buzzard," the malevolent element from the psychosocial environment (the buzzard) interacted with Tad's conscious self (*eni*). Because the African chief betrayed his people by helping whites enslave thousands of Africans, the Great Master decided that the chief was lower than all of the animals and humans and caused his spirit to wander endlessly in the form of a buzzard. The Great Master is part of the religio-spiritual sphere. This tale involves the total person (Tad) as a self-in-the-universe. Furthermore, Tad ensured the health of the self because he was afraid that the buzzard would harm him. He recalled that the air seemed like poison, and the buzzard was trying to vomit on him. When Tad ran, the buzzard circled around and tried to tackle him. Everywhere that the buzzard vomited the grass dried up and died. Eventually, Tad escaped in order to avoid possible harmful influence from the buzzard.

In "Transmigration," the owl (the spirit of Ole Man Smart Daniel's Daddy) is the malevolent element in the psychosocial environment that interacted with Tad's *eni*. Tad's grandfather, whom the owl mentioned, functions in the realm of the religio-spiritual sphere (ancestral spirit) and also interacted with Tad's *eni*. As was the case with "The King Buzzard," this analysis of "Transmigration" involves Tad as a self-in-the-universe. Moreover, the situation of ensuring the well being of the self is demonstrated through Tad's interaction with the owl. Tad listened to the owl, but he did not remain with the spirit long. The owl wanted to whisper a spirit world sign into Tad's ear and walked toward him, but Tad immediately broke the spell. Tad did not want a spirit world sign or further interaction with the owl/spirit. By breaking the spell, Tad prevented/neutralized harmful influences from the malevolent element of the psychosocial environment. Tad's actions ensured the health of the self.

Another significant concept in the Ifa literary corpus is reincarnation, an idea that is connected to the theory of the Seven Heavens. Both concept and theory are part of the worldview projected in "The King Buzzard" and "Transmigration." In the Ifa tradition, death is not thought of as death at all:

> Apart from the disappearance of *ara* (body) into dust, the soul as the indestructible element of a person must continue to exist either in the form of a spirit or reincarnated in a different body in a different place, or reborn again into the same family. (Makinde 38)

Ajalorun (Olodumare, Olofin, Orun, Olorun, Eledaa, Oda Igbehin, Oba Aiku, God) is the giver of new life after death. Ajalorun lives in the seventh and last heaven and, at the time of reincarnation, receives reports about a person's activities in her/his life. Just and unjust souls are judged based on their deeds on Earth. The *Iko* or *Iranse* (ambassador/messenger) reports "on individual human activities through each of the seven heavens" (Makinde 40-41). Reincarnation takes place in the seventh heaven. Ajalorun is the only one who commands the kind of life an individual will live, depending on her/his previous life:

> Thus the soul of a wicked person may be caused to enter into the body of a snake, a tree or a goat while the soul of an oppressed person or a slave may be caused to enter into the body of a king or queen. In all cases, the soul of just persons are rewarded with the possibility of good life after death while those of unjust persons are ably punished by being re-incarnated in the forms of some despicable beings or the other. (Makinde 43)

In "The King Buzzard" and "Transmigration," the spirits of unjust people are reincarnated into despicable beings. The spirit of the African chief is reincarnated into the form of an enormous buzzard, a punishment determined by the Great Master. I interpret the "Great Master" as a reference to Ajalorun because the two entities function in the same manner. Since the African chief sold his people into slavery and killed their spirits, the Great Master (Ajalorun) punished him in a number of ways. The chief's spirit must wander for eternity over the face of the Earth, travel in the form of a buzzard, eat only carrion as his food, never touch a living thing with his beak and claw, and travel alone. The reincarnation of the African chief would have taken place in the seventh and last heaven where Ajalorun lives.

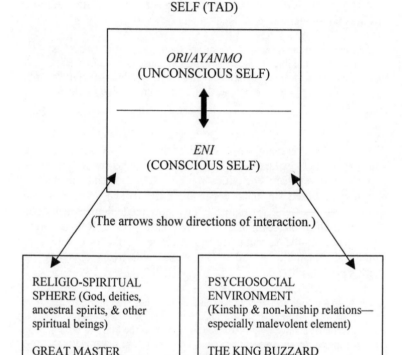

Diagram of the Dynamics of the Self and Tad as a Self-in-the-Universe Based on "The King Buzzard" and "Transmigration."[19]

"The King Buzzard" also reflects the belief that the soul is indestructible. Tom mentioned that life continues after the disappearance of the *ara* and that in the spirit world this buzzard was known as the King Buzzard.

In "Transmigration," the soul of Ole Man Smart Daniel's Daddy was reincarnated into the form of an owl as punishment for living inappropriately in the world. The owl explained that he could not rest or tolerate daylight. As with "The King Buzzard," the reincarnation in "Transmigration" would have taken place in the seventh heaven where Ajalorun receives reports about the person's life and activities and judges her/his soul. Also reflected in "Transmigration" is the belief that the soul is the indestructible element of a person. The owl tried to give Tad a spirit world sign that would enable Tad and the owl to recognize each other after Tad died, an action that points to the belief in the continuation of life after the *ara* disappears. The owl also observed that some people live in the form of different animals, and when that animal is killed, the individual changes form again, comments that suggest the indestructible nature of the soul.

The Ifa worldview (as reflected through the Ifa concepts of self-in-the-universe and reincarnation) projected in "The King Buzzard" and "Transmigration" indicate one's social relationship to the spiritual domain. The tales express the self in relation to evil and misfortune. In addition, there is a continuing interactive relationship among the living, the spirits, the dead ancestors, and the *ajogun* in the two folktales. I speculate that numerous enslaved Africans in South Carolina had this view of themselves in the universe, a worldview that was part of their private thoughts and was encoded in these tales and passed on from one generation to the next through the oral tradition.

"The Yellow Crane" and Agbigbo

Similar to "The King Buzzard" and "Transmigration," "The Yellow Crane" uses bird imagery to project hidden meanings. However, in "The Yellow Crane" that imagery is connected to Black slaveholders. Relatively little information is available about Black slaveholders in the United States and even less is known about how enslaved Africans perceived them. "The Yellow Crane" is one folktale in which the issue is represented. Using the Ifa concept of Agbigbo, the tale deals with 19th century Black slaveholders in South Carolina.

In "The Yellow Crane," Saber and Limus had been fishing at Crane Lake when a huge yellow crane confronted them—the bird was taller than a man. Limus died during the encounter. The crane had eyes like a goose and an extremely long bill and looked like an old man with a yellow beard (as well as the father of death). An evil spirit appeared to be gazing through the side of the crane's head. The crane walked over to Limus, stepped on him, and then walked across the swamp. Kike explained that the crane was actually the spirit of a dead man named Issue. Free Issues (people who had a Black father and white mother during slavery) enticed Black people to Crane Lake.

Issue was a doctor who lived on Crane Lake and killed Blacks but did not harm whites. He looked like a crane and wore a long black cloak. When Issue was a child, his father sent him to a foreign country to go to school and brought him back after he had completed his studies. That Issue's father sent him to medical school abroad (as his contemporary, aristocratic white neighbors would have) indicates that his father was a rich Black man. Furthermore, that Issue killed Blacks (indicating that Issue, like a slaveholder, had the power of life or death over Black people), I believe symbolizes that he was a slaveowner, as was the case for the relatively few rich, free Blacks whose economic status set them apart from other Black people, as well as above the laws which applied to most Black people during the antebellum period in North America.

As early as 1790, the Black community in South Carolina was divided between slave and free people as well as between mulatto and Black in Charleston City. The "mulattoes of Charleston sought to maintain what they perceived as a special relationship with the white aristocracy and separated themselves from the majority of Afro-Americans, attempting a distinctly separate class" (Koger 168). In 1850, there were 184 black slaveowners in Charleston. Mulattoes represented 85.4% (or 157) of these slaveowners in 1850 while 14.6% (or 27) were dark-skinned masters (Koger 171). Many of these well-to-do free Blacks also owned houses and plantations; "owning land and slaves, the Negro elite could not be confused with slaves, who were regarded as the lowest in the Southern social order" (Koger 167).

Rochefoucauld Liancourt, who visited America in 1795-97, observed a rich Black man who owned an estate in South Carolina:

> In the township of St. Paul a free negro, who from his early youth carefully stored up the produce of his industry, possesses a plantation of two hundred slaves. [. . . Such] a plantation is here a phenomenon. The severity excepted, with which this emancipated slave treats his negroes, his conduct is said to be regular and good. His name is Pindaim, and he is eighty-five years old. He has married a white woman, and has given his daughter, a mulatto, to a white man. (602)

Koger also discussed the man who Rochefoucauld Liancourt referred to as "Pindaim." The wealth of Pindaim "appears to be the dominant factor which facilitated his entrance into the white world" (Koger 13). Pindaim's actual name was James Pendarvis. He was a free person of color and slaveowner "from St. Paul's Parish in Charleston District as the Duke recalled. [. . . However,] according to the first federal census, Pendarvis owned 123 slaves and not 200 slaves" (Koger 13).

Although relatively few in number, there was a group of rich Black slaveholders in South Carolina, a reality that "The Yellow Crane" deals with through the Ifa concept of Agbigbo. In *ese* Ifa, the Agbigbo bird is portrayed as evil and "regarded as a treacherous and dangerous bird who acts as an agent for death and other supernatural powers" (Abimbola, *Ifa* 211). If Agbigbo places a coffin in front of someone's house that person will die. Agbigbo is also regarded as a negative Ifa priest who deceives and cheats clients. "The Agbigbo bird is therefore the symbol of unfaithfulness in Ifa priests, a negation of the strict sanctions of the Ifa divination system" (Abimbola, *Sixteen Great Poems of Ifa* 210). The parallels between Agbigbo and the Yellow Crane reflect the connection between the two birds. Agbigbo carried a load of evil on his head, and the Yellow Crane looked evil and an evil spirit gazed through the side of his head. Also, Agbigbo and the Yellow Crane functioned as agents for death. If Agbigbo placed a coffin in front of anyone's house that person would die. Similarly, when the Yellow Crane appeared, a Black person nearby always died. Moreover, the Yellow Crane looked like the father of death. Furthermore, both birds represent a male who was unfaithful to his profession. Agbigbo was an unfaithful Ifa priest, and the Yellow Crane was a doctor who killed, rather than healed, Blacks. There seems to be bird substitution in "The Yellow Crane." An Agbigbo bird is a Grey Hornbill or Allied Hornbill, but in the folktale the evil, treacherous bird is a yellow crane. There were no hornbills in South Carolina or North America, a fact that would help to explain the bird substitution.

Since in 1850 about 157 of the 184 Black slaveowners in Charleston City were mulattoes, Issue could very well symbolize this group of individuals. The reference in the tale to Issues as a new race of goose-eyed Blacks who had minds and ways of their own could represent the mulatto class in South Carolina who felt that they were a separate race and who disassociated themselves from slaves and other Blacks. "The Yellow Crane" reveals how people from the Ifa tradition treated the South Carolinian reality of Black slaveowners, a situation that is expressed symbolically. Issue becomes Agbigbo, a treacherous, dangerous, and evil bird who acts as an agent of death. The folktale critiques and condemns Issue and reflects the disdain that the slaves felt toward Issue (and by extension all Black slaveowners). The enslaved Africans maintained and transmitted these culturally distinctive ideas in spite of the harsh conditions of slavery.

Notes

[1]From 1830 to 1840, between twenty and thirty thousand slaves escaped the South. An estimated fifty thousand fugitive slaves were in Canada alone in 1855. (Starling 39)

[2]Pater-rollers were white people who acted as type of police force over the enslaved Africans. The law prohibited pater-rollers from killing slaves because the enslaved Blacks were considered valuable property to their owners. However, they could whip and brutalize slaves for any reason. The pater-rollers' tyranny added to the agony of enslaved Africans. (Faulkner 29)

[3]Sometimes before these meetings enslaved Africans would also "turn a pot down so as not to let the sound go to far. [It was an ancient African practice to invert a large cooking pot or wash pot in the belief that it would capture secret conversations]" (Hurmence *We Lived in a Little Cabin* 65). See also Faulkner, *The Days When the Animals Talked*; Botkin, *Lay My Burden Down*; Mellon, *Bullwhip Days*.

[4]Harriet Jacobs, who had been a slave in North Carolina, recalled that after Nat Turner's revolt in Southampton County, Virginia (1831), slaves in North Carolina could not meet together, the church in the woods that the slaves had built was destroyed, and "visiting was strictly forbidden on the plantations" (Jacobs 67).

[5]For an account of the Stono Rebellion and the impact that rebellion, as well as other slave revolts, had on South Carolina, see Wood, *Black Majority*.

[6]For more information about the slave revolt on the *Creole*, see Jones, "The Peculiar Institution and National Honor: The Case of the *Creole* Slave Revolt." Douglass's historical novella *The Heroic Slave* (1853) is an imaginative account of Madison Washington's life. Douglass also discusses Washington in several of Douglass's speeches including "American Prejudice Against Color: An Address Delivered in Cork, Ireland, 23 October 1845," "America's Compromise with Slavery and the Abolitionists' Work: An Address Delivered in Paisley, Scotland, on 6 April 1846," and "American and Scottish Prejudice Against the Slave: An Address Delivered in Edinburgh, Scotland, on 1 May 1846" (reprinted in *The Frederick Douglass Papers Volume 1: 1841-46*). In his 1843 speech at the National Negro Convention, Henry Highland Garnet described Washington as a "bright star of freedom."

[7]The following sections of this chapter are based on two of my articles which were published in the *CLA Journal*: "The Yellow Crane/Agbigbo: A Critique of Black Slaveholders" (1996) and "Encoding and Decoding: The Ifa Worldview in 'The King Buzzard' and 'Transmigration'" (1997).

[8]This *ese* Ifa is sometimes referred to as "How Agbigbo Bird Acquired the Pad on Its Head."

[9]Orunmila is a representative of the divine forces.

[10]Previously, Orunmila killed Agbigbo's father and asked Agbigbo to bury his father.

[11]Esu (Eshu-Elegba) is the Yoruba trickster god who receives all sacrifices offered to the gods. He punishes those who refuse to perform sacrifices and rewards those who perform sacrifices. In this *ese* Ifa, Agbigbo was the only one who did not perform sacrifice.

[12]Agbigbo-niwonran is Agbigbo's full name.

[13]Abimbola argued that "although the various branches of the Ifa literary corpus do not conform with any branches of modern academic knowledge,

this should not detract from its importance as a body of knowledge" ("Ifa as a Body of Knowledge" 1).

[14]See Abimbola, *Ifa: An Exposition* and *Sixteen Great Poems of Ifa*; Bascom, *Ifa Divination*; and Johnson, *The History of the Yorubas* who discuss Ifa as part of the cultural milieu of the people from the Lower Guinea cultural zone.

[15]The Yoruba oral tradition also provides information about the origin of Ifa divination. According to one narrative, the deity Ifa and other divine beings first landed in the city of Ife after leaving heaven to establish order on Earth:

> Ifa played a major role in the divine ordering because of his great wisdom. At this period of sojourn of Ifa at Ife, he lived in a place known as Oke Igeti. That is why one of his praise names is *Okunrin kukuru Oke Igeti* (the small man of Igeti Hill). [. . .] We also learn in these myths that Ifa had eight children and a number of disciples, all of whom he taught the secrets of divination. (Abimbola, *Ifa* 4-7)

Ifa's children used sixteen palm-nuts known as *ikin* (that Ifa had given them) for divination. "The sixteen palm-nuts were the symbol of the authority by Ifa to his children to continue making divination in his absence. [Ifa had gone back to heaven]" (Abimbola, *Ifa* 4-7).

In *History of the Yoruba*, Samuel Johnson discussed another narrative concerning the origin of Ifa divination, according to which a blind Nupe man named Setilu introduced Ifa to Yorubaland. When he was a child, Setilu would foretell who would visit his parents' house. As he "advanced in age, he began to practice sorcery and medicine. At the commencement of his practice, he used 16 small pebbles" (Johnson 33). People flocked to him for consultations about their problems. However, the Muslims of Nupe expelled Setilu from the country. After staying in Owo and Ado, Setilu migrated to Ile Ife and decided to stay there. He soon became famous:

> Setilu initiated several of his followers in the mysteries of Ifa worship, and it has gradually become the consulting oracle of the whole Yoruba nation. In order to become an Ifa priest, a long course of serious study is necessary. [. . .]
> Ifa was really met in this country by the Yorubas, for ODUDUWA [the legendary ancestor of the Yourba people] met Setilu at Ile Ife, but the worship of it was officially recognized by KING OFIRAN son of ONIGBOGI. (Johnson 33-35)

Johnson's account would place the official recognition of Ifa about the 12th or 13th century.

[16]Frank Willett in *African Art* described a wooden tray collected at the Ardra Kingdom in 1659 that was used in Ifa divination.

[17]For detailed discussion about the numbers of enslaved Africans from the Lower Guinea cultural zone who were brought to South Carolina, see Curtin, *The Atlantic Slave Trade: A Census*; Inikori, *Forced Migration*; and Pollitzer, "The Relationship of the Gullah-Speaking People of Coastal South Carolina and Georgia to Their African Ancestors."

[18]Among the *ajogun* are *Iku* (Death), *Arun* (Disease), *Egba* (Paralysis), and *Ofo* (Loss). This placement of the buzzard in "The King Buzzard" within the *ajogun* is a departure from the symbolism of the vulture in the Ifa literary corpus. While the worldview in "The King Buzzard" is Ifa, the vulture symbolism indicates another African influence, a point that I am currently investigating. In Ifa, the vulture (*Igun*) is associated with prospects of living to an old age, and *Igun* plays a significant role in Ifa divination sacrifice. *Igun* helps in making sacrifices accepted by eating them. In fact, according to *ese* Ifa, "without igun, nobody performs sacrifice" (Abimbola, *Sixteen Great Poems of Ifa* 28-29). This variant between the vulture symbolism in "The King Buzzard" and that in the Ifa literary corpus reflects the multiple African influences within the tale.

[19]This diagram is adapted from Morakinyo 76.

Chapter 3

Asante Icons in *Sankofa*[1]

Birds are the primary symbols in "The King Buzzard," "Transmigration," and "The Yellow Crane" through which the historical and cultural dimensions of the narratives are revealed. The birds simultaneously represent Ifa, specific historical events, and people. They are also symbols of memory and slavery. As with the three oral narratives, *Sankofa* utilizes bird imagery and signs (in this case those of Asante culture) to image history. Extending techniques of the oral tradition into film while often transforming them, *Sankofa* (similar to the folktales) brings to life elements of African and African American history.

An insistent theme in Haile Gerima's work is "transformation, change, realization" (Howard 29). Mona, the main character in *Sankofa*,[2] is clearly transformed as a result being transported to the past to experience slavery, and she breaks the cycle of a passive existence. Furthermore, the film's focus on individual identities and motives of characters is a point of radical departure from the plantation school of literature and cinema, in which enslaved Africans are represented as a happy and docile group who talk similarly, have no human dimensions, and whose "identity is fully determined by the context of the plantation" (Woolford 92). In *Sankofa*, the history of slavery is full of resistance and rebellion. The viewpoint throughout most of the film is that of the private elements of the slave community (secret societies, whispered messages, coded signs, secret meetings, brief interactions) where plans for rebellion transpire. In addition to this privatized sphere which frames the narrative of the past, a parallel realm exists in the film, one which in some ways provides further insight into Mona's journey (her shifting subject position in the realm of the visual) and in other ways is independent of that narrative. This other dimension is a coded domain, projected through Asante cultural markers. In this chapter, I explore the relationships between the Asante signs and women in *Sankofa*. My discussion is structured around two areas: (1) the *sankofa* symbol and the buzzard; and (2) Nunu and Asona ancestors.

Sankofa & the Buzzard

The central Akan symbol in the film is that of *sankofa* (the image is of a bird with its head turned so that its beak touches its back). In Akan, the term and symbol mean *se wo were fi na wosankofa a yenkyi* (it is no taboo to return to fetch something which has been forgotten)--return to the past in order to go forward. While the image of *sankofa* is in the center of the screen, there is a voice-over of Gerima's poem "Spirit of the Dead." The symbol and poem foreshadow Mona's journey, for soon she will return to her past, and the spirit of the dead will tell their story.

Drums can be heard throughout the opening scene in the background then in the forefront. The camera angle moves from Mona to the Divine Drummer (Sankofa) who is a self-appointed guardian of Cape Coast Castle in Ghana, West Africa and communicates with the spirit of the dead with his drums. Every morning he wakes up at sunrise, goes to the foot of the final exit of the castle[3] with his drums, casts his net across the ocean, and communicates with the spirit of the dead ancestors. At sunset, he faces the west beating his drums. He holds the staff with the *sankofa* symbol as the *okyeame*[4] among the Asante (and the Akan in general) would carry a staff with a symbol (generally based on a proverb) of the state s/he represents. "Indeed, the proverbs communicated by their symbols are often an iconic capsule of official policy respecting a given situation" (Yankah 33). When the Divine Drummer approaches Mona, he transfers the staff from his right hand, a movement that the *okyeame* would have made to gesture when s/he was about to pronounce judgment. Sankofa is going to pass judgment on Mona who has been selected to return and discover her African ancestry. The staff is a symbol of the Divine Drummer's authority, as well as a key "to indigenous systems of indirect communication" (Yankah 33). The images shift from Sankofa to the buzzard, the *bird of passage* in the poem, indicating the link between the two as architects of Mona's journey. The *sankofa* symbol then occupies the screen before a close up of the Divine Drummer who points the staff at Mona. The symbol announces his presence and his decision for Mona to return to her past. The buzzard[5] waits for this judgment and throughout the film the buzzard is present--watching, planning, as well as absorbing the scene, the people, and especially Mona waiting for the moment to take her to an American sugar plantation during the slave era. Once the journey begins, the camera focuses on the sky where the buzzard soars. Simultaneously, sounds of the slave ship forcing its way through the ocean and slaves being whipped echo below the clouds. An image of the buzzard landing is juxtaposed with that of Mona whom the buzzard has placed on the Lafayette Plantation as a house slave named Shola. Shola/Mona does not speak of this first encounter with the buzzard, an experience that seems to have been buried in her subconscious.

However, after the second slave revolt when Shola and the other slaves are running toward the hills (toward freedom), Shola describes her second encounter with the buzzard. She is running as fast as she can, but the slaveowners and dogs are catching up to her. Suddenly, she feels light (the pain in her feet ceases), and she realizes that a buzzard is carrying her in the air back to Africa. The image in the film is of being carried over the ocean. Only with the buzzard's cooperation is the journey possible, for he takes people to the past and returns them to the present.[6] After the buzzard brings Mona back to Africa, the camera centers on the *sankofa* symbol, marking the end of Mona's journey. She has returned to the past and can now move forward. While the buzzard flies over Cape Coast Castle, Mona joins the Divine Drummer and other Blacks who have made the journey. The closing images of the film are the buzzard, Mona, the ocean, and then the buzzard. The film ends as it began with the voice-over of "Spirit of the Dead."

That the buzzard took Shola/Mona away from slavery and to safety recalls a legend in Dutch Guiana. Africans in Dutch Guiana consider the buzzard sacred because the sacred vulture, *opete*,[7]

> carried one of their warrior ancestors away from slavery across the river and into the bush. [. . .] Bush and town invoke the buzzard, *Opete*, so named in Ashanti [. . .] and the style of

> dancing resembles certain of the dances of the 'saints' who 'shout'
> in the Negro Sanctified Churches of the United States.
> (Herskovits, *Rebel Destiny* x)

When dancing for the buzzard, the people "went about in a circle, moving with bodies bent forward from their waists and with arms thrown back in imitation of the birds from which their spirit took its name" (Herskovits, *Rebel Destiny* 330).

A link can be made between the representation of the buzzard in *Sankofa* and traditional beliefs about vultures in some places in West Africa including Sierra Leone, Dahomey, and Nigeria. In Dahomey and in Limba society in Sierra Leone, for example, vultures play a significant role in sacrifice. Suvinenge (vulture-child nenge), one of the gods of the Earth pantheon in Dahomey, is connected to sacrifice. "It is not believed that Suvinenge is really a vulture, but he is held to resemble the largest of these birds, having a bald head and being of a dark grey color" (Herskovits, *Dahomey* 140). Suvinenge has the head of a man and the body of a vulture. "It is this deity who is believed to indicate whether or not sacrifices are acceptable to the gods, for when sacrifices are offered, and they disappear after being left overnight, it is thought that Suvinenge has taken them to the deity for whom they were intended" (Herskovits, *Dahomey* 140). One of the ways (and the most important) that the living and dead communicate in Limba society in Sierra Leone is through sacrifice (*saraka*). The vultures which come after a sacrifice "are seen as a sign that the dead have accepted [the people's] prayer" (Finnegan 20).

In Benin and Yoruba art of Nigeria, the vulture symbolizes "the mothers" (Jeffries 116). Furthermore, there are three dimensions of meaning of engraved vultures in 14th century Nigerian Bronze rings, objects that are linked to the city of Ife during the classical period:

> On one level, they are real vultures of the sort that can be seen in
> African towns. [. . .] On another level, they allude to the correct
> accomplishment of ritual, and to acceptance of sacrifices by the
> gods in the person of Vulture, their messenger. On a third level,
> they are a reference to the "mothers," the elderly women with
> special hidden powers without whom mortuary and installation
> rites for kings cannot be completed. (Vogel 61)

In the Niger Delta, the vulture spirit is Fene-Ma-So, bird of the sky and the king of birds (Talbot 87-88). When the vultures appear after a sacrifice has been made to Fene-Ma-So, it is believed that he accepted the sacrifice.

A connection can also be made between these beliefs about vultures and the "buzzard lope dance" (which "is a close imitation of the bird"[8]) in various southern states in North America. The buzzard lope dance was known throughout the South, during as well as after slavery, and is connected to West African beliefs about the sacred status of the vulture (Stearns 26). The dance in Georgia as performed by the Johnsons (a family on Sapelo Island in Georgia) is described below:

> Naomi did the patting while Isaac did the dancing; an older brother rhythmically called out the cues in a sharp staccato, and another one lay on the floor of the wide veranda representing a dead cow.
> [The song that accompanied the dance follows:]
> March aroun'! (the cow)
> Jump across! (See if she's daid)
> Get the eye! (always go for that first)
> So glad! (Cow daid)
> Get the guts! (They like em' next best)
> Go to eatin' (on the meat)
> All right!--cow mos' gone!
> Dog comin!
> Scare the dog!
> Look aroun' for mo' meat!
> All right!--Belly full!
> --Goin' to tell the res'. (Parrish 111)

"Dances simulating the peculiar characteristic of animals are popular in Africa; and Mr. Herskovits tells me [Lydia Parrish] that he has seen a similar dance in Dahomey" (Parrish 108). I speculate that the dance that Herskovits observed in Dahomey was connected to the beliefs about Suvinenge discussed previously.

Through *Sankofa's* personification of the buzzard, the film seems to create a link to these traditional West African beliefs and others like them about vultures, as well as symbolize the ways in which these traditions continued in North America. The buzzard is positioned as sacred in the film and an architect for the journey to the past. The Divine Drummer communicates with the ancestors, and their messenger, the buzzard, arrives to accept the sacrifice. In the context of the film, the sacrifice is the individual (Mona) who will be taken to the past. By the end of the film, the *sankofa* symbol acquires additional meanings established through a scene when Shango, Shola's lover, gives her a handmade bird he carved from wood his father had given to him. He called it a *sankofa* bird and put it around her neck. Shola recalls that she became a rebel after Shango gave her the bird, and she joins the secret society of the plantation and participates in the second slave revolt. Hence, the symbol becomes associated with rebellion and slave resistance, as well as Shola/Mona's transformations. For Shola, change meant participating in a slave revolt, while Mona connects with her African ancestry and disassociates herself from the media that defines Black people through a Eurocentric framework. These scenes are markers for shifts in Shola/Mona's subject position. The implication at the end of the film is that Mona will define herself and the role she will play in society.

Nunu & Asona Ancestors

In *Sankofa*, Nunu preserves the oral tradition and the traditional beliefs of the enslaved Africans. Nunu is an African-born slave on the Lafayatte Plantation, an Asante, a symbol of supernatural power, and leader of the secret society of the plantation. Shola describes Nunu as all strength, passion, and tenderness and feels that Nunu was part of her memory/past. In spirit, Nunu still lives in Africa. She commands great power in her eyes--to heal or kill. One day she kills an overseer just by staring at him. Nunu is also the keeper of the oral tradition and history. Shola observes that she was as excited as the children to hear Nunu's stories from Africa, and Shola would run and find a seat near the fire. In one scene, Nunu is surrounded by children and several adults as she tells a story about the porcupines and Afree (a name that means "special") the little porcupine girl. The porcupine girl loved her family, and they loved and protected her. Her mother, a powerful medicine woman, created medicine from roots, herbs, and plants to heal people. Afree's father, a warrior, predicted that Afree would be a seer. In another scene when Nunu is braiding Shola's hair, Nunu continues the story of the porcupine girl. When Afree was fourteen years old, she was taken by whites and enslaved. On the slave ship, the men and women were separated, and a white man raped Afree.

As is characteristic of African oral narratives, the experiences of the animal characters in Nunu's stories represent events in the "real" world and are "introduced partly to entertain [the audience] and partly also because the experiences of these animals are meant to have some relevance or message. [. . .] The audience is expected to derive meaning from the events narrated" (Okpewho 104 and 181). The events contained in tales set in the world of animals have meaning if treated as symbols illustrating certain aspects of the problems and issues surrounding life in the world of humans. Nunu uses her stories to describe her experiences among the Asante in West Africa--Afree is Nunu. She gives the audience a place to remember (their home, origin), as well as people to remember (the family members who they were ripped away from when enslaved). Nunu's stories of Afree also serve as a way for her to deal with and reveal to Shola the most painful, traumatic, and horrifying moments of her past. When she was fourteen years old, a white man on the slave ship raped Nunu. She became pregnant as a result of the rape, and her son Joe was born.

Nunu's command of the oral tradition also manifests itself during secret meetings of the enslaved Africans. In a code embedded in a chant that Nunu recites during an initiation ceremony of the secret society, there is a message that points to specific historical moments in Asante history—(1) an ancient time of the founding of the Asante clans; and (2) the Yaa Asantewaa War. In the caves away from the plantation, Nunu chants/sings her coded message in which she requests that the spirits of Asona[9] ancestors join them and drink, and she thanks these spirits for bringing everyone to the meeting safely. She then asks the spirit of Prempeh[10] to eat and drink with them. Like the buzzard who expands the context of the film through time and space by moving in and through historical moments, Nunu's references to Asona and Prempeh mark movements in and through time as well as highlight critical junctures in Asante history, although at the time of the action in the film some of the events have not yet happened. Hence, as the buzzard does, Nunu transcends time by communicating not only with the African ancestors but also with future generations of Asante.

Asona is the name for one of the Asante clans. According to the "History of Ejisu" in the *Ashanti Stool Histories*,

> From time immemorial the Ejisus have belonged to the royal Asona tribe. Tradition has it that it was an elephant that brought the Asona tribe from the ground into the world at a place called Adaboye, which is commonly known as Abuakwa. The elephant emerged with a woman called Asoh Boade. [. . . When Asoh Boade died, she] was succeeded by her daughter, Dokuwah, as the Queen-Mother of the Asona tribe. (Nkansah 1)

In addition, Ejisu is the birthplace of Yaa Asantewaa (born between 1840 & 1860), the Queenmother[11] of Ejisu and leader of Asante opposition against the British in a war that bears her name--the Yaa Asantewaa War (1900-1901). Like the other descendants of Ejisu, Yaa Asantewaa belonged to the royal Asona people. Furthermore, when Nunu evokes the name of Prempeh she also points to the historical moments that link to Yaa Asantewaa. Prempeh I, Asantehene, was enstooled[12] in June 1894. In 1896, the British Imperialists arrested him and exiled him in the Seychelles Islands with other members of the royal family. Leadership of the Asante Empire fell to Yaa Asantewaa.

> She hated the British for their shabby treatment of Prempeh and her son [Nana Afrane Kuma who the British had exiled with Prempeh] and during the four years after the establishment of the British Residency in Kumasi she built up Asante hatred for the strangers in their midst. (Sweetman 87)

On March 28, 1900, the British Governor of the Gold Coast, Frederick Hodgson called a meeting of all of the kings in and around the city of Kumasi.

> He informed the people that their exiled King Prempeh would not be permitted to return. He reminded them that the indemnity that the British had demanded before the exile of King Prempeh had not been paid. Further, he demanded that the Ashanti surrender the Golden Stool [--the supreme symbol of the sovereignty and independence of the Asante . . .]. The governor in no way understood the sacred significance of the Stool, which, according to tradition, contained the soul [Sunsum[13]] of the Ashanti. (Clarke 132)

The Asante left the meeting in silence and, inspired and led by Yaa Asantewaa, prepared for war. The Asante continued to fight, but eventually Yaa Asantewaa and her chiefs were captured. In May 1901, she was sent into exile in the Seychelles Islands where she died in 1921. She remains a symbol of Asante resistance to British colonization and "because her agitation for the return of Prempeh was converted into stirring demands for independence, it is safe to say that she helped to create part of the theoretical basis for the political emergence of modern Africa" (Clarke 133).

At the Yaa Asantewaa House, a large compound in the center of the town of Ejisu in Ghana, Afia Tweneboah (the head of the household and great grand daughter of Yaa Asantewaa) and Tweneboah's children keep the memory of Yaa Asantewaa alive through the oral tradition. According to Tweneboah, when Yaa Asantewaa was younger, she lived in a village not far from the modern-day Yaa Asantewaa House in Ejisu, a compound into which she moved after she became Queenmother of Ejisu (she about 50 years old). When the British demanded the Golden Stool, Yaa Asantewaa was the only one to stand up and say that the Asante would not comply. In a private meeting of the chiefs and kings, she announced that she would lead the fight against the British as the War Marshall. The kings and chiefs supported her. She participated in all of the fighting. Other women participated in the war by drumming and singing to encourage the warriors into battle. These songs and the echo of the songs would travel with the warriors and stay in their minds giving the warriors strength to fight. People remember Yaa Asantewaa as a strong, bold, and courageous woman. She is also remembered through praise songs, and in Ghanaian school exams in history, questions about Yaa Asantewaa and the Yaa Asantewaa War are included. In addition to discussing the history of her ancestor with me, Afia Tweneboah showed me pictures of Yaa Asantewaa, sang praise songs for her, and poured libations for me in Yaa Asantewaa's name. Yaa Asantewaa epitomizes all that is brave, courageous, and purposeful. Songs about her are popular, as well as praises including: *Yaa Asantewaa the woman who fought that war because of anger. She was annoyed*; and *the woman who was not subdued by the gun.*

The reference to Asona juxtaposed with that of Prempeh in *Sankofa* is a sign for a critical moment in Asante history--the Yaa Asantewaa War. This juxtaposition complements the theme of resistance in *Sankofa*, but in the historical situation the fight was against British colonization. Asante war against the British began in 1805; hence, the Yaa Asantewaa War marks nearly 100 years of resistance. A parallel can also be drawn between the image of Nunu preparing for battle and the representation of Yaa Asantewaa in a praise song, and I would argue that Nunu symbolizes Yaa Asantewaa. In one scene in *Sankofa*, Nunu, with machete in hand, leads the warriors (women and men) into battle on the plantation calling out to the warriors to rise up, an image which recalls the following praise for Yaa Asantewaa, "Yaa Asantewaa, the warrior woman who carries a gun and a sword of state in battle" (Sweetman 90).[14]

The "History of Ejisu" from the *Ashanti Stool Histories* also reflects Asante cosmogony, according to which women founded the various Asante clans, as Asoh Boade founded the people of Ejisu. Other examples of such origin narratives include those of Amoaful, Anyinase, and Juaben, which provide a glimpse into the history projected in *Sankofa* through Nunu's chant. The Amoaful Stool is a stool of matrilineal descent and belongs to the Bretuo matri-clan:

> Tradition asserts that the ancestress of the royal Bretuo Clan Asiama Nyankonpon Ghahyia came down from the sky by a silver chain known as Atwiaban. [. . .] Before her arrival a bird called Afwia announced, 'Ene, bribi bebe kuro yi mu,' (something strange is about to happen in this village today). Then followed a leopard, Kurotwiamansa. And then from the sky came Asiama Guahyia with the silver stool and with her relatives and subjects. (Agyeman-Duah 2 and 4)

Nana Ebena Baa Panin is the ancestress of the Anyinase Stool. She came down from the sky through a silver chain (Atwiaban) with other members of the Oyoko Clan and her own ancestral stool. She settled at Akim Asiakwa (present-day Southern Ghana). They migrated to several different locations then became residents of Kokofu Adweso, a village about 20 miles from Kumasi. Later, Nana Ebena Baa Panin died at Kokofu Adweso and was succeeded on the stool by Nana Ago, her sister.

The ancestress of the Juaben Paramount Stool is Aberewa Ampim. She settled at Otikurom Juaben Mma (Small Juaben) and stayed there for about four or five years. Much later, Nana Juaben Serwah [the 12th Chief of Juaben] arrived at Juaben:

> Nana Fredua Agyeman gave her [Juaben Serwah] a certain gold ornament, by name Kanta (regalia, bracelet, chain or necklace), elevating her to the position of a Female Paramount Chief. Nana Serwah spent eight years on the Stool after leaving Obo. (Agyeman-Duah 6-7)

She was succeeded by her daughter, Afrakumah Panyin (the 13th Chief of Juaben), who reigned as Paramount Chief. Nana Afrakumah Panyin spent almost 12 years on the Stool and was succeeded by Nana Sapoma (the 14th Chief of Juaben).

The origin narratives in the *Ashanti Stool Histories* accentuate the tradition of *ohemma* and female chiefs among the Asante:

The importance of women in Asante government is shown by the fact that a new asantehene [Asante king] was selected by the queen mother, in consultation with certain advisors, from among her daughter's sons or her daughter's daughter's sons. From earliest times, in different Akan states, the queen mother had ruled when the king died or was deposed and no successor had been appointed. There are legends of women rulers leading their warriors into battle. (Sweetman 85)

Furthermore, the Akan *ohemma* "holds her title because of her seniority in the royal matrilineage and not because of any relation to a particular male" (Farrar 585). The queenmother is still significant in Asante culture today, although she does not hold the same political power as she did in pre-colonial Ghana.

Female chiefs are also part of Asante culture. In the Juaben Paramount Stool History, for instance, the 12th, 13th, and 14th chiefs were women--Nana Juaben Serwah, Nana Afrakumah Panyin, and Nana Akua Sapoma. Contemporary examples of female chiefs include the chief of Agona Nsaba traditional area who "was a woman up to a few years ago, and so is the chief of Ekumfi Atwia, a village in the central region of Ghana" (Yankah 71). A two-layered story unfolds around Nunu: (1) the narrative of Nunu as oral historian, preserver of traditional African religions, leader of the enslaved Africans and of slave revolts, embodiment of supernatural power; and (2) the narratives of women in traditional Asante culture which are projected through Nunu's chants. This second layer is linked to the women who founded the Asante clans, the *ohemma* (especially Yaa Asantewaa), and female chiefs.

By focusing *Sankofa* on women as active agents of change in history and warriors in the fight against oppression and linking those ideas with Asante cosmogony in which women have significant leadership positions, the film disrupts the Eurocentric thinking that assumes

that humans have progressed from matriarchy to patriarchy, in a kind of universal transition from darkness to light, the reign of women being symbolized by darkness and the reign of men by light. This is a classic case of Eurocentric thinking--the use of dichotomy; hierarchical ranking; the positive valorization of those characteristics that most parallel European culture; the demeaning of the place of women; and finally, the ascription of all of this to the universal proclivity of human beings. (Monges 127)

This type of Eurocentric thinking has been naturalized and constructed as the non-political norm. Ways of thinking and viewing the world that do not align with that mode of thought have been deemed insignificant and trivial--the "other" relegated to an inferior position to the superior "norm." However, *Sankofa* represents another worldview connected to traditional Asante culture in which Black women are central in and through history. Mona's journey puts her in contact with part of the memory of her past, Nunu who (through her chant) opens a window into Asante cosmogony, creating a network that ties Mona to the spirits of Asona, as well as the spirits of the women who founded the Asante clans, *ohemma*, and female chiefs.

Notes

[1]This chapter is based on my article "'Spirits of Asona Ancestors Come:' Reading Asante Signs in Haile Gerima's *Sankofa*" which was published in the *CLA Journal* (1998).

[2]The term *sankofa* is an Akan word that means return to the past in order to go forward.

[3]The final exit of the castle was the "door of no return" for the enslaved Africans. This exit was an extremely narrow doorway--there was only enough room for one person to pass through at a time. A small boat waited beneath the exit to take the enslaved Africans to the slave ship that was a short distance from the castle.

[4]*Okyeame* is the Akan word for royal spokesperson. The *okyeame* put the chief's or king's words into eloquent language and was an ambassador and a prominent person at the royal court.

[5]Among the Akan, "the scarab and the vulture symbolize self-begetting, self-creation and self-birth. An Akan maxim says of *Odomankoma* [the infinite, interminable, absolute being]: 'The animal that symbolizes Odomankoma who created the world is the vulture' (*Odomankoma a oboadee, ne kyeneboa ne opete*)" (Meyerowitz, *The Divine Kingship in Ghana and Ancient Egypt*). See also Danquah, *The Akan Doctrine of God*.

[6]After Nunu was killed late in the film, no one could find her body. Shola says that people believed that Nunu did not die; rather a buzzard swooped down and took her back to Africa.

[7]*Opete* is the Akan word for vulture.

[8]Marshall and Jean Stearns 35. See also *Drums and Shadows* 176.

[9]Asona is the name of one of the Asante clans.

[10]Prempeh I was *Asantehene*, King of Asante, 1888-1931 (exiled 1896-1924).

[11]In Akan, the word for queenmother is *ohemma* ("female ruler"), a woman who wielded true political power in pre-colonial Ghana and could assume full control of central authority.

[12]The word "stool" is often used to "indicate the office of the chief and the king" (Sarpong 33).

[13]"The Akans distinguish between the *Sunsum*, that is the personality, character, energy and *Akra*, which is the individual soul which enters the body at conception and leaves after death. It was the *Sunsum* of the nation that was contained in the stool, not the aggregate of their *Akra*" (Sarpong 77-78).

Moreover, the Golden Stool is a symbol of nationhood and contains the *Sunsum* or soul of Ashanti:

> The Golden Stool is considered to be so sacred that no person whatsoever is allowed to sit upon it. It is kept with the strictest security and precaution; and is taken outside only on exceptionally grand occasions. Never must it come in contact with earth or ground. It is always lying on its own stool or on the skin of an animal such as the leopard. Ashantis have on many occasions made great sacrifices to defend it when its safety had been threatened. (Sarpong 32)

[14]See also Farrar 579-597.

Chapter 4

Orisha & Codes in *Daughters of the Dust*

Integral to both *Sankofa* and *Daughters of the Dust* is the interweaving of the verbal, visual, and symbolic to represent the experiences of enslaved Africans and to create narratives on a firm historical foundation. Through the buzzard and the journey, Mona gains memories of slavery in *Sankofa*, while in *Daughters of the Dust* (set in 1902) the slave era is in the recent past, and many of the characters represent former slaves--their experiences in the antebellum South alive in their memories. In *Sankofa*, the viewer witnesses a re-creation of slavery through Mona reliving the events of Shola's life. In *Daughters of the Dust*, flashbacks and oral narratives about slavery open the door to the antebellum South for the viewer. The story in *Daughters of the Dust*, however, is framed around the descendants of the enslaved Africans and their desire to leave the South for what they view as a utopia North. Similar to *Sankofa*, *Daughters of the Dust* relies on codes to project traditional African belief systems.

Through the creation of *Daughters of the Dust*, Julie Dash functions as a *jelimuso* (a term, used in Mande traditions in West Africa, which refers to a female hereditary professional historian and musician who preserves and presents history through the oral tradition). However, Dash transforms that role in the landscape of the South Carolina Sea Islands by projecting, through the medium of film, new symbols which represent experiences of enslaved Africans and their descendants in North America.   The film is set on one of the Sea Islands in South Carolina on the last day the Peazant family spends on the Island, a region which seems "storied since the beginning of time" (Baker 164).   Nana Peazant and Eula are the voices of the past, as well as the primary keepers of the oral tradition. The narrative structure is based on the way griots recount stories.   In order to break with cliché, formula, and stereotype in representing the history of enslaved Africans in North America, Dash used numerous symbols in *Daughters of the Dust* including the figurehead of an African warrior floating in the swamp, ancient markings within drawings on the wall, and a graveyard that reflects burial practices of the Kongo.   The viewer sees these images without commentary for, as Dash explained, dialogue sometimes diminishes objects (Baker 164-165).   Dash described three levels of viewers of *Daughters of the Dust*—insiders who are knowledgeable about the African and African American historical/cultural material in the film; others who are not knowledgeable about (or interested in) the historical/cultural material, yet the story continues; those who are unfamiliar with the material in the film but want to study the subject (Baker 165). The first idea that Dash described, what I call *being within the circle,* signifies on the encoding strategy (as exemplified in the tales "The King Buzzard," "Transmigration," and "The Yellow Crane") used by enslaved Africans--the individual had to be within the circle of the slave community *to know.* However, in her comments, Dash included openness to the discovery of the deep levels of cultural and historical material within her film.

This chapter is concerned with *Daughters of the Dust*'s coded use of a network of *orisha* (Yoruba deities) including Yemaya (Yemoja), Oshun, Oya, Ogun, and Eshu-Elegba (Esu).   The first clue to the code can be found in handwritten notes in the film script; however, as with the images Dash projects in the film to break with cliché, formula, and stereotype, there is no commentary about the Yoruba/character pairs (Yellow Mary/Yemaya, Trula/Oshun, Eula/Oya, Eli/Ogun, Unborn Child/Eshu-Elegba, Nana Peazant/Obatala).[1]   *Daughters of the Dust* builds on what the *orisha* are in the Yoruba system of belief yet creates something new in the context of the film.   In contemplating the pattern of the *orisha*/character pairs in *Daughters of the Dust*, I found that the significance of the code can be found by exploring the pairs in the following contexts: (1) the Yoruba river goddesses (Yemaya, Oshun, and Oya) and their connection to ideas about women in traditional Yoruba culture; (2) the interplay among the *orisha*/character pairs as a marker for specificity of African cultures.

Yemaya, Oshun, Oya & Alternative
Traditions for Black Women

In the beginning of *Daughters of the Dust*, Yellow Mary and Trula arrive in a boat and join Eula, a scene that seems to represent a symbolic reunion (as well as the power) of Yemaya, Oshun, and Oya. The three characters are pictured together walking along (or sitting near) the water throughout much of the film, an appropriate place since their *orisha* counterparts are river goddesses.

Yemaya, mother of all rivers in Yorubaland, is the river goddess noted for her use of a round fan. An artistic strategy by those who worship the river goddesses is the "use of the round fan as an emblem embodying the coolness and command of these spirits of the water" (Thompson, *Flash of the Spirit* 72). She (along with other river goddesses) is supreme in the arts of mystic retribution and protection against all evil (Thompson, *Flash of the Spirit* 73-74).[2] Yemaya's strength is alluded to in the following excerpt from an *ese* Ifa: "Yemoja, the wind that whirls with force into the land. Yemoja, angered water that smashes down the metal bridge" (Thompson, *Flash of the Spirit* 75). River goddesses are often visualized as women with swords.

Oshun is "the giver of children, the leader of the *aje*, [. . .] a wealthy and beautiful woman, an herbalist and dyer," as well as a diviner who learned the *merindinlogun*, sixteen-cowries divination, from Orunmila, the Ifa deity of wisdom and knowledge (Badejo 1). She takes charge of the profession/art of hairplaiting and hair dressing (her nickname is Sheegesi, "the Hair Expert with the Beaded Comb"):[3]

> Oshun is believed to have the power to influence the destinies of men and gods, orisha, for better or for worse. Oshun's presence is crucial to the sustenance of life and order on earth. She is the source of potency for most if not all male-dominated cults like the Egungun "ancestral masquerades," Oro "the collective male dead, whose voice is the bull-roarer", Gelede "to honour our mothers" and Ifa the Yoruba divination deity. (Abiodun 3)

She reigns in glory at the bottom of the Osun River.

According to *ese* Ifa, seventeen Odu (one woman--Oshun--and sixteen men) came from heaven to earth. The men would not do anything for Oshun, although they did many things for each other including preparing a grove and making a home. However because they did not honor Oshun, they had no success. Death, sickness, and drought threatened them. Eventually, the sixteen male Odu went to heaven to Olodumare who told them that if they did not honor Oshun their problems would not be solved, and he warned them: "If you continue in this way, you will always fail" (Abiodun 6). After their conversation with Olodumare, they realized (and admitted to Oshun) that all Odu derived from Oshun, and their suffering would continue if they failed to recognize and obey her. Oshun, whose name means "the vital source," is the seventeenth Odu with whom the destinies of the remaining sixteen male Odu rested, and she is essential to a successful political, economic, religious, and social life. Her praises include:

> She is the wisdom of the forest
> She is the wisdom of the river
> Where the doctor failed
> She cures with fresh water.
> Where medicine is impotent
> She cures with cool water. (Abiodun 33)

Oya is the goddess of the whirlwind and the Niger River. Shango (the third king of the Yoruba who became the god of thunder and lighting) wanted to marry Oya. He consulted Ifa who told him that Oya would be stronger than Shango, so he refused to offer sacrifices to Ifa because he could not accept the fact that Oya would be stronger. However, Oya, who controls strong winds including hurricanes and tornadoes, is stronger than Shango. Oya and Shango worked well together as rulers of Oyo (as well as husband and wife) and later became *orisha*; "they have been working together ever since. Incidence of strong winds, tornadoes, and hurricanes are always" heralded by thunder and lighting (Abimbola, Adetokunbo 22).

In traditional Yoruba belief, without the sanction of women

> no healing can take place, rain cannot fall, plants cannot bear fruit and children cannot come into the world. [. . .] Yoruba tradition also suggests that women of any age are potential witches who possess *eye*, the "bird power" given them at creation.

[*Eye* like *ase*, a form of prophetic power, enables women to accomplish anything.] The recognition of this extraordinary power by society has caused men to appease women "our mothers" (Iya wa Osoronga), a term used synonymously with "witches" (*aje*). (Abiodun 7)

Aje are not necessarily negative; rather the term means unusual power or extremely intelligent--to have bird power is to have extraordinary power/knowledge.

Ero, "a soothing,. disarming and softening kind of power [. . .] which is capable of normalizing, negating, or rendering impotent any other power, life, or substance," is another kind of power that women have (Abiodun 12-13):

Like water, *ero* operates noiselessly and unceremoniously. [. . .] Whatever enables women to extinguish life [. . .] without any visible or materially attributable force, presupposes her fore-knowledge of the metaphysical principles of life including its source. [. . .] With the power of *ero* which can be either positive or negative in effect, women are not only feared, but their cooperation is sought in all endeavors. Without their cooperation, nothing would be possible. (Abiodun 12-13)[4]

In traditional Yoruba society, women's power and authority also came through leadership roles. For example, women were *alaafin* (rulers) who controlled central authority and even founded Yoruba polities. For example, a woman (one of Oduduwa's[5] daughters) founded Ketu. Although there are no female kings[6] today, "the decision by women not to compete with the men for the kingship was of their own volition, not imposed by the men" (Lawal 267). Women also held (and in some cases still hold) other important political positions in Yoruba polities, including *iyalode* (a term that can be translated as "older anafemale in charge of public affairs" and is someone in charge of the markets who had authority over the community's economy, regulating supply and demand, product pricing, allocation of stalls, tolls, fees, and fines), *baale* (village head), and chieftaincy titles *arise* and *lobun* (Oyewumi 96, 108-109).

The association of Yellow Mary, Trula, and Eula with three Yoruba river goddesses (and thus traditional beliefs about women in Yoruba culture) undermines Eurocentric notions that women are always (and in all cultures) passive, powerless, and subjugated to and demeaned by men. Furthermore, Haagar and Yellow Mary represent two polarized ideas about women's roles in society. Haagar valorizes those characteristics that most parallel European culture and therefore wants to forget her African heritage, traditions and beliefs that she disparages. She feels that she is moving into a "new world" up North where there will be no need for traditional African beliefs or Nana's magic. Haagar does not want her children to hear about traditional African beliefs. She also feels that women belong in the kitchen. Early in the film when Haagar tells Yellow Mary that women who can cook are beautiful, she places feminine beauty (as well as women's place) within the domain of the kitchen (and by extension family/mother/wife), a traditional European framework. However, it is evident when Yellow Mary tells Haagar that she does not like being in the kitchen or cooking that Yellow Mary rejects certain types of domesticity (Dash 67). Moreover, Yellow Mary represents something different from the equation Haagar establishes (beauty equals cooking/family/mother/wife). The Cousin describes Yellow Mary as a scary (not a family) woman, but Myown asserts that Yellow Mary is a new type of woman. Indeed, Yellow Mary is "new" in the sense that she is different from what Haagar, Myown, and Cousin are familiar with. However, as a symbol of Yemaya, Yellow Mary represents an ancient Yoruba figure. Furthermore, Trula and Eula, as symbols of Oshun and Oya, also represent ancient Yoruba deities, as well as offer an alternative tradition with different views about women, one focused on power as represented by Yemaya, Oshun, and Oya.

By juxtaposing these Yoruba deities with Yellow Mary, Trula, and Eula, Dash suggests other ways of viewing the characters' subject positions. This point is exemplified when Eula addresses the "daughters." She begins her address by looking to the past and recalling that the "daughters" believe that the Peazant women (the female elders and ancestors who had been slaves) were ruined when the white slaveholders raped them, that the Black women's wounds cannot be healed, nor can the women be protected from the world that enslaved them. Eula employs what Bell Hooks called counter-memory:

> Looking and looking back, Black women involve ourselves in a process whereby we see our history as counter-memory, and use it as a way to know the present and invent the future. (*Black Looks* 302)

In order to know the present, Eula recalls the horror of rape and sexual exploitation out of which the former slave women came.

While white men extolled the white woman as the "nobler half of humanity" and depicted her as a goddess who was virtuous, pure, and innocent (Hooks, *Ain't I a Woman?* 31), they defined Black women as "instruments guaranteeing the growth of the slave labor force" (Davis 6). Black women were "victims of sexual abuse and other barbarous mistreatment that could only be inflicted on women" (Davis 6). Harriet Jacobs, a former slave, explained that slave women were "entirely unprotected by law or custom," and the laws reduced them to "the condition of a chattel, entirely subjected to the will of another" (55). Eula contemplates this history to know her present in which the legacy of such sexual exploitation is evident in her and Yellow Mary's circumstances in that white men raped both Eula and Yellow Mary. After looking back, she looks forward by encouraging the Peazant women to transform their way of thinking before leaving for the North, honor the ancestors, embrace and love Yellow Mary, and remember that they are good women. Eula's way to create the future starts with the mind. The Peazant women must first change their way of thinking (move out of the Eurocentric construct of viewing women). They are the daughters of the slaves who came before them, as well as the descendants of Africans including Yoruba and BaKongo. Eula suggests that they remember the past but not be consumed by it. She confronts history then looks to the future and presents ways to decolonize the mind, to move away from the construct that positions Black women as "ruined," and toward the system in which Black women possess *eye* and *ero* and have the power to create the future.

Orisha & Specificity

The strategic interplay among the *orisha*/character pairs in *Daughters of the Dust* points to the ancient Yoruba belief system and marks the specificity of African cultures, providing a counter effect to the project of colonialism which, in part, was the erasure of such specificity. "For the colonist, the Negro was neither an Angolan nor a Nigerian, for he simply spoke of 'the Negro'" (Fanon, *The Wretched of the Earth* 211). Rather than perpetuating that kind of negation, *Daughters of the Dust* emphasizes ancient Yoruba traditions through a network of *orisha* which indicate specificity. The film speaks, often through sign, of the Yoruba, Igbo, Kongo, and more. The references to/symbols of specific African people in the film represent ancient African nations.

The subtexts of the *orisha* Ogun and Eshu-Elegba are played out in the film through water and wind and are interwoven with those of the Yoruba river goddesses in that Yemaya, Oshun, and Oya reign over water, and Oya commands strong winds. Moreover, in traditional Yoruba belief, "the power of women appears to be similar to that of water, with which most female deities are associated" (Abiodun 11). Throughout *Daughters of the Dust* water is in the background of most scenes and is the space for triumphs, as well as tragedies. On the bank of Ibo Landing, for instance, Eula recounts the success of the Igbos who walked on water back to Africa and freedom. After these Igbos walked off of the slave ship, they looked around, saw what was going to happen to them in the future, turned around, and walked toward the water. With iron chains on their ankles, wrists, and necks, the Igbo men, women, and children walked on water back to Africa. After completing this narrative, Eula opens her arms and Unborn Child returns to her womb marking the completion of Unborn Child's mission.

In and near water/Ibo Landing is also the site of several powerful experiences for Eli (Eula's husband), a blacksmith who represents Ogun, the Yoruba deity of war and iron. Ogun "lives in the flames of the blacksmith's forge, on the battlefield, and more particularly on the cutting edge of iron" (Thompson, *Flash of the Spirit* 52). Part of a praise song for Ogun is "Ogun, master of the world, support of the newborn child" (Thompson, *Flash of the Spirit* 52). This praise song is relevant to Eli in that he will become, as Ogun already is, the support of the newborn child. Under the guidance of a spirit-rider, Eli is able to walk on water--the precursor to his accepting the Unborn Child, for he has seen that she is his. Furthermore, the healing between Eula and Eli transpires on the water's edge.

The water is also the site of tragedies including the slave girl who was drowned by her master and Bilal's account of Ibo Landing. Unlike Eula's narrative, according to Bilal's the Igbo drowned. This association among triumph, tragedy, and water can also be seen in Yoruba narratives. In one legend, for example,

> two round droplets of water remaining in the mouth of a single fish reconstitute the peace that brought back order into the world. [. . . However,] the coolness of the riverain goddesses is problematic. Vengeance, doom, and danger also lurk within the

holy depths (*ibu*) of the rivers where the goddesses are believed
to dwell. (Thompson, *Flash of the Spirit* 73)

In *Daughters of the Dust*, the wind is primarily connected to
Unborn Child whose arrival is marked by a great gust of wind.
Similar to Eshu-Elegba, Unborn Child represents the crossroads and
is a messenger. Eshu-Elegba "came to be regarded as the very
embodiment of the crossroads" (Thompson, *Flash of the Spirit* 18):

> According to legend, at a crossroads in the history of the Yoruba
> gods, when each wished to find out who, under God, was
> supreme, all the deities made their way to heaven, each bearing a
> rich sacrificial offering on his or her head. All save one. Eshu-
> Elegbara, wisely honoring beforehand the deity of divination
> with a sacrifice, had been told by him what to bring to heaven--a
> single crimson parrot feather (*ekodide*), positioned upright upon
> his forehead, to signify that he was not to carry burdens on his
> head. Responding to the fiery flashing of the parrot feather, the
> very seal of supernatural force and *ashe*, God granted Eshu the
> force to make all things happen and multiply (*ashe*). (Thompson,
> *Flash of the Spirit* 18)[7]

Eshu-Elegba is also the messenger of the gods, "not only carrying
sacrifices, deposited at crucial points of intersection, to the goddesses
and to the gods, but sometimes bearing the crossroads to us in verbal
form" (Thompson, *Flash of the Spirit* 19). Furthermore, Eshu has the
ability to turn himself into wind for quick travel. In one *ese* Ifa, for
instance, Eshu turned into wind to go to the city of Ikoolo so that he
could punish Agbigbo for not performing sacrifice.[8] Similar to Eshu,
Unborn Child travels as wind to deliver a message, although hers is
not one of punishment. She is a messenger on a spiritual mission and
symbolizes the crossroads through her parents Eula and Eli. When
the strong winds begin to blow that mark the arrival of Unborn Child,
Nana (who preserves and shares the secrets and wisdom of the
African ancestors) turns her face into the wind and welcomes Unborn
Child. Nana had prayed for her arrival. Daddy Mac links the sudden
wind to the breath of a baby. The African ancestors send Unborn
Child with a message to her parents who are at the crossroads of
leaving the Sea Island or staying and for Eli of staying with Eula after
a white man raped her and believing that the child she carries is Eli's.
Unborn Child is successful in her mission for Eli learns that she is his
child, and Eula and Eli decide to stay on the Sea Island close to the
African ancestors, rather than go North with the other family

members. Yellow Mary also remains on the island. Unborn Child observes that everyone who stayed on the island grew stronger and wiser.

Daughters of the Dust, Black Thunder, & the Kongo

Another marker for specificity in *Daughters of the Dust* is the Kongo, a topic I discuss briefly in this section in relation to Arna Bontemps's novel *Black Thunder* (1936). This reading focuses on the primary Kongo symbols reflected in the film and novel (four moments of the sun, *booka* gesture, and *mwelo* between two worlds). During one moment in *Daughters of the Dust*, the camera zooms in on a turtle shell on which someone has drawn the sign of the four moments of the sun, a symbol that connects the people to traditional Kongo beliefs in West Africa. The four moments of the sun are dawn, noon, sunset, and midnight. When it is midnight in the world of the living, the sun is shining in the world of the dead. (Thompson, *Four Moments of the Sun* 27). "The Kongo cosmogram mirrors the birth of a person, in the rising of the sun; the maximal power in a vertical line which culminates with the sun at noon; the death and decline in the lowering of the sun and its disappearance beneath the sea or earth" (Thompson, *Four Moments of the Sun* 43).

Other Kongo symbols are revealed in *Black Thunder* during the funeral for Bundy, the slave who is savagely beaten to death by his master. As the funeral scene commences, the narrator emphasizes that in 1800 the slaves remembered Africa. Hence, Africa is established as a symbol of home and origin for the slaves before the funeral begins. The slaves perform an African burial to send Bundy to the land of the dead and to the slaves' ancestors and to ensure that his spirit will not haunt the living. The mourners (facing the sun, hands--with fingers apart--in the air, and kneeling) begin to sing without words (Bontemps 52). The mourners in *Black Thunder* also have their faces to the sun, the sun was in the west, and the word *sun* is repeated about five times in the scene, phrases which are also significant. Most rituals and initiations in the Kongo take the pattern of the circle of the sun about the Earth. Given the relevance of the sun in the Kongo cosmogram and the importance of circles in many West African ceremonies, it seems clear that the sun (and looking toward the sun) is significant in the African burial detailed in *Black Thunder*. In Kongo terms, the reference to the sun signifies the life cycle. At the end of the scene, the sun is far in the west lowering and disappearing, movements which mean death and decline in the Kongo construct. Since the implication in the scene is that Bundy receives a proper burial, his spirit will join the dead ancestors.

Another Kongo influence in the scene is the mourners' hand gestures. During the burial, their hands (with fingers apart) were in the air, a *booka* gesture according to Thompson:

> *Booka* refers to holding both hands above the head, fingers wide apart. The word refers to crying out for help, weeping, and proclaiming. (Thompson, *Four Moments of the Sun* 176)

Also of importance in this scene in *Black Thunder* is the reference to Ben, an old slave owned by Mr. Moseley Sheppard, kneeling down (and joining the singing and moaning) at the meeting place of the two worlds (53). Similarly, in early scenes in *Daughters of the Dust*, Nana Peazant can be seen kneeling near a grave in the cemetery and talking with the dead ancestors. The cemetery, in traditional Kongo belief, is

> a door *(mwelo)* between two worlds, a "threshold" marking the line between the two worlds, of the living and the dead, circumscribed by the cosmic journey of the sun. (Thompson, *Four Moments of the Sun* 27)

Furthermore, in the Kongo, "the graves were the principal medium through which the living communicated with the dead" (Hilton 11). Hence, the reference in *Black Thunder* to where Ben kneels and scenes in *Daughters of the Dust* with Nana in the cemetery indicate that Ben and Nana Peazant are at the threshold where the world of the living and the world of the dead meet and show the close connection that the living have with the dead in the novel and film.

The use of Kongo symbols without comment in *Daughters of the Dust* and *Black Thunder* recalls the encoding strategy used among enslaved Africans in North America during the antebellum period. However, the technique has been transformed in the film and novel, for the Kongo symbols are projected to, as well as intended for, large audiences. The Kongo influences in *Daughters of the Dust* and *Black Thunder* represent Black people asserting themselves by practicing West African traditions.

Orisha & Viewing the Past

The Yoruba river goddesses (and by extension Yellow Mary, Trula, and Eula) signify another tradition (another way of viewing/knowing) through which Black women can relate uninterrupted by Eurocentric notions of women as passive and powerless in all cultures and at all times. The Yoruba river goddesses represent women with *eye* and *ero* who were active agents of change in and through history. They are women who operate like water, are often more powerful than men, and have the power to heal.

Furthermore, the intricate interaction among all of the *orisha* who are part of the subtexts/codes in *Daughters of the Dust* points to the ancient Yoruba belief system and marks the specificity of African cultures. The film suggests that the viewer look back and (re)discover/recognize the traditional beliefs in and rich histories of African nations and people, rather than perpetuate the idea that in looking back one finds darkness and/or empty space. *Daughters of the Dust* suggests that to begin to decolonize the mind calls for people to look back with scholarly eyes as they look forward--to recognize/remember/recover the history destroyed, distorted, and disfigured by colonialism.

Notes

[1]For handwritten notes see Dash, *Daughters of the Dust: The Making of an African American Woman's Film*.

[2]See also Thompson, *Black Gods and Kings: Yoruba Art at UCLA*.

[3]"The hairplaiter/dresser is seen as one who honours and beautifies Ori-inu, lit. 'inner head', the 'divinity' of the Head, also taken to be the visible representation of one's destiny and the essence of one's personality" (Abiodun 3). See also Thompson, *Flash of the Spirit* 79-83.

[4]See also Beier, "Gelede Masks" 5-24.

[5]Oduduwa was the first king of Oyo.

[6]The phrase "female king" has been used to refer to women who ruled in Yorubaland because in English the connotation of "king" is the highest position of authority in the nation (one who controls central authority), while the "queen" is the king's wife. For discussion of female kings in Yorubaland, see Oyewumi, *The Invention of Women* and Lawal, *The Gelede Spectacle and Social Harmony in an African Culture*.

[7]*Ashe* is "spiritual command, the power-to-make-things-happen, God's own enabling light rendered accessible to men and women. The supreme deity, God Almighty, is called in Yoruba Olorun, master of the skies. Olorun is neither male nor female but a vital force. In other words, Olorun is the supreme quintessence of *ashe*" (Thompson, *Flash of the Spirit* 5).

[8]For more details regarding this *ese* Ifa about Agbigbo, see Chapter 2 of *Symbolizing the Past* ("History, Memory, & the African American Oral Tradition" 10-11).

Chapter 5

Mirroring Narrative/ Reflecting Past:
Eve's Bayou, Tradition, Preservation

Moving from *Sankofa* and *Daughters of the Dust* to *Eve's Bayou* brings the viewer forward in time. However, the opening images in *Eve's Bayou* alert the viewer to the narrative's link to slavery in North America. That the film is framed by the historical reality of slavery is clearly established when, in a voice-over, the narrator tells the story of Eve, an enslaved African woman who had the power to see the future and to heal, supernatural abilities that her female descendants inherited from her. As they were in *Sankofa* and *Daughters of the Dust*, symbols are integral to the narrative structure in *Eve's Bayou*. A recurring motif in *Eve's Bayou* is that of African American women as keepers of the oral tradition--through Black women, the generations learn about their history, as well as inherit supernatural power.

Eve's Bayou, a film set in Louisiana, opens with a series of black and white images that bridge the past and the present and symbolize the power of sight, for it is through black and white images that the women with supernatural power see the future and past. While the narrator speaks of her African ancestor Eve, the camera moves through sugar cane fields and slave cabins on a plantation. The camera stops on a path where an enslaved African woman, Eve, fades into the scene and stands on the path between the sugar cane. She walks a few steps, and the viewer sees the bayou with over grown trees and a variety of plants near the edge of and over the water. Eve, standing near the edge of the bayou, raises her right arm in front of her (as if to point to the future generations on which the film focuses), and the narrator proclaims that her family members are the descendants of Eve and Jean Paul Batiste. The young Eve was named after her African ancestor. The camera moves in the direction that Eve points, and the screen shifts from black and white to color, a change that indicates a movement in space and time. Starting with *Eve's Bayou*, this chapter explores representations of Black women as preservers of the oral tradition & possessors of supernatural power then considers the history (as well as living tradition) of Black women storytellers in North America.

The African Ancestor: Inheriting Her Power

At Eve's request, her aunt (Mozelle Batiste-Delacroix) brings to life the story of Maynard (one of her husbands) and Josiah (her lover). A captivated Eve is caught up in the interplay between the verbal and visual unfolding of the oral narrative. As Mozelle speaks the narrative, the two men appear in a full-length mirror. Entering the mirror and the re-created scene, Mozelle relives that moment/memory with these two men. Ever engaging the audience, Mozelle directly addresses the internal textual audience (Eve) and by extension the viewers to emphasize certain points in the story. Eve observes the action in the mirror. Unexpectedly, Josiah arrives at Mozelle's house and tells Mozelle to pack because he is taking her with him. Mozelle immediately starts to walk upstairs to pack then stops when she hears Maynard, in a tone she has never heard before, tell her lover to leave the house. Gun in hand and aimed at Maynard, Josiah announces that he is in love with Mozelle and will kill Maynard if he tries to stop them. Pushing his chest into the barrel of the gun, Maynard informs Josiah that he will have to shoot because Mozelle is not leaving. At that moment realizing that she loves Maynard, Mozelle stands with her husband and tells Josiah, the man who had lit a great fire in her, to leave. Josiah agrees to leave then shoots Maynard in the chest, and Mozelle is alone.

A gifted oral historian as well as a seer, Mozelle literally and figuratively brings to life that narrative. The mirror becomes a window into the past, rather than a reflection of the self. She reveals part of her history and shares it. Her role in the film is similar to that of the *jelimuso* in Mande traditions in West Africa. The *jelimuso* (like the *jeli*) is the memory of the people and brings to life that memory through the oral tradition. Similarly, Mozelle functions as the family historian who inherited the gift of sight from her African ancestor, Eve. Even when she was ten, Mozelle could look at strangers and clearly see their lives. Her ancestor Eve was a slave who saved her master's (General Jean Paul Batiste) life using powerful medicine when he was stricken with cholera. In gratitude (and in return for his life), he freed her and gave her some land by the bayou. She later had 16 children with him.[1] The town in which Eve's descendants live is named after her. In addition to being a skilled healer, Eve was a seer. Both Mozelle and her niece Eve inherit their special power from their African ancestor Eve.

Mozelle's power to see the future is well know in the community of Eve's Bayou. "Clients" come to her for information, guidance, and help. For a fee, she provides them with the information they seek. After the client asks Mozelle a question, she prays to God, takes her/his hands, and sees the subject of the client's inquiry. The images Mozelle views during the counseling sessions are in black and white and in the following order--scenes of the bayou, the person and information sought, the bayou. Her ability is far reaching, and she is able to give detailed accounts. In some cases, she also turns to voodoo. In one scene, for instance, Mozelle decides to give a client named Louise, whose niece spent all of Louise's money, specific instructions to create a "hand" (a small bag of special ingredients which Louise is to keep next to her skin for protection). Mozelle does not charge her for the session. As Mozelle walks Eve home after that counseling session, Eve queries Mozelle about her use of voodoo and reminds her that she told Louis that she does not practice voodoo. Her aunt explains that the woman was desperate. The voodoo seems to have worked (or at least Louise is convinced that it will work) for in a later scene when Louis, who is Louise's doctor, is on his rounds and visits her, she assures him that everything is fine. After he leaves, she takes out the "hand" that she wears close to her skin as instructed and pats it with satisfaction.

Although Mozelle can view other people's lives very clearly, she laments that she is unable to see her own life. She looked at each one of her husbands, who all died tragically, and never saw their futures. As a result of her husbands' deaths and her barrenness, Mozelle believes that she is cursed. Near the end of the film, however, the implication (as evidenced through a dream she describes) is that the curse is broken. In the dream, she was flying, and she saw a drowning woman (herself). The air that enabled Mozelle to live was killing her duplicate. While contemplating whether or not to save the drowning woman, she heard Louis advise her to continue forward, so she kept flying. The other woman (Mozelle's other self) died. In the morning, Mozelle agrees to marry Julian Grayraven who seems to help Mozelle overcome her own pain. Julian first came to Mozelle seeking information about his wife who left him a year earlier. Julian stays with Mozelle (leaving only briefly to get a divorce from his wife who has another lover), and he and Mozelle fall in love. In a scene that follows one in which Mozelle and Julian are together, Eve is at home looking at a black widow spider through a windowpane. Throughout the film the image of the black widow is juxtaposed with Mozelle, especially in relation to the deaths of her husbands, implying that she, like the black widow, kills her mates. The juxtaposition of the spider with a scene of Mozelle and Julian implies that he too will die. However, Mozelle's dream seems to indicate that her curse is over--that the woman drowning was her former, cursed self while a new, healthy self survives. Julian seems to be an important part of the process through which Mozelle heals. He tells her that she is not barren; rather she is wounded in her heart. He assures her that he will heal her heart.

In addition to Mozelle's inability to see her own life, in times of emotional distress her interpretation of images she receives can be clouded, indicating another limit of her abilities. In a moment of anger after an encounter with Elorza (a fortune-teller in town), for example, she misinterprets images connected to one of Roz's children. Mozelle is infuriated because of the fortune that Elzora reveals (that Mozelle will always be a cursed, black widow) and runs across the street in front of a bus marked "Eve's Bayou." When looking at the bus destination sign, she sees a man walking down train tracks and a child fall then she faints. She has actually seen Lenny Mereaux shoot Louis because Louis was having an affair with Lenny's wife Matty; as the train passes by, Louis pushes Eve out of the way when he sees Lenny's gun. However, in her emotional distress coupled with her and Roz's misinterpretation of Elzora's warning when Elzora read Roz's fortune, Mozelle believes that she has seen one of Roz's children hit by a bus. During Roz's fortune-telling session (prior to Mozelle's), Elzora advises Roz to look to her children. Mozelle and Roz believe that Mozelle's vision and Elzora's warning to look to the children are linked. In response to what she perceives as a dangerous arena (the outdoors) that poses a threat to her children, Roz locks them in the house in spite of Louis's protests. In support of Roz's decision, Gran Mere (Louis's mother) says that her generation appreciated warnings and signs, a comment directed at Louis who does not believe in the signs. When Roz finds out that a neighbor's child was hit by a bus, she releases her children from the house.

Effectively acting on Elzora's warning, however, would involve much more than merely locking the children inside. No one in the family seems to be attending to the children's emotional and psychological states. Louis's escapades with numerous women in town, his neglect of his family, the constant fighting among the adults (especially between Roz and Louis), and Roz's apparent inability to deal with the breakdown of her family, severely affects the children as evidenced in their growing anger, depression, and hostile (as well as violent) behavior. The children, for the most part, must look after themselves and to each other for emotional support.

In spite of the turmoil in the Batiste family, Eve's supernatural ability flourishes in the film. Like Mozelle, Eve inherits her African ancestor's power. The first indication of her special ability is revealed early in the film when (in a dream) Eve sees the following images that indicate that Harry (Mozelle's third husband) will die in a car crash: a grandfather clock, a black widow spider, scenes from the party (Harry taking pictures, Harry giving her a coin), a tombstone, coins spinning, Harry in the car, a car crash, a black widow spider killing its mate (an image which foreshadows Elzora's accusation that Mozelle is a black widow), the red brake light of a car. Eve wakes up and discovers that Harry died the night he left the Batiste party.

The scene in which it is clear that Eve not only has her ancestor's name but also her power of sight[2] occurs near the end of the film when Eve confronts Cisely. Previously, Eve believed, without question, Cisely's account of Louis's actions (that, on the night of the storm, Louis kissed Cisely inappropriately then slapped her when she resisted his advances). Eve vowed to kill Louis (which she attempts to accomplish with the help of Elzora and voodoo). However, Eve discovers Louis's account of that night in a letter Louis wrote to Mozelle. In that letter, Louis said that he did not violate Cisely. He was drunk when Cisely kissed him, and he realized that she was kissing him like a woman (not like a daughter). Because he was shocked, he slapped her. However, before he could talk to her, she ran. An irate Eve confronts Cisely first by calling her a liar then by demanding that she reveal what actually happened. After Cisely admits that she is unable to recount the events, Eve puts out her hands (palms facing up). Eve's hand gesture recalls an earlier scene when Mozelle requires that Eve do the same after Eve inquires about using voodoo to kill someone (a moment which also reflects a difference in motives for using voodoo--while Mozelle is interested in voodoo to heal, Eve seeks that same knowledge to kill). In response to Eve's query, Mozelle demands to know why Eve would want such information then requires that Eve put out her hands. Mozelle catches Eve's secret (the incident between Cisely and Louis) but drops Eve's hands in shock. Mozelle later confronts Louis and accuses him of violating Cisely, a confrontation that he refers to in his letter addressed to Mozelle, the same letter that Eve finds on his desk.

Cisely puts her hands on Eve's, and Eve sees images of the night of the storm. However, since Cisely is confused about the events (she genuinely does not know what happened), Eve is unable to determine the meaning of the images. They put the letter in the bayou, push it down with a stick, and watch as it sinks to the bottom of the bayou. In the voice-over that closes the film, an adult Eve acknowledges her power of sight and links images with memory. The story comes full circle when it closes with the narrator voicing the words with which the film began. She explains that some images are illusive, while others are printed permanently on the brain. After reviewing the events of that summer as an adult, Eve changes her position on the cause of her father's death. She revises her initial statement from *the summer I killed my father I was ten* to *the summer my father said goodnight*. This shift from Eve as subject (*I killed*) to Louis as subject (*My father said goodnight*) places the action and responsibility on Eve's father (Louis left). Apparently, Eve realizes that even though she used voodoo on Louis and although Lenny pulled the trigger, Louis's lifestyle is what ultimately killed him. The responsibility rests with Louis.

Throughout *Eve's Bayou*, future and past events are a series of images. The interpretation of those images is tied to the state of the seer when she views them. In a moment of emotional distress, for example, Mozelle misinterprets the images she receives about the falling child. In Cisely's confusion and Eve's anger, Eve is unable to obtain concrete meaning from the images of the night of the storm. However during times of clarity, images, events, and interpretations are crystal, and memory is indeed history and that history is tied to the power of sight in *Eve's Bayou*. Eve represents the next generation in the film, but she is also inextricably connected to her African ancestor Eve from whom she inherits her power.

Eve's Bayou can be placed within a larger tradition of fiction by African American women in which the motif of supernatural power emanating from Black women and being transmitted to their descendants recurs, works which include *Mama Day* (Gloria Naylor), *Daughters of the Dust: A Novel* (Julie Dash), and *Wildseed* (Octavia Butler). Mama Day and Cocoa, for example, gain their supernatural powers from Sapphira Wade, a conjure woman who has the power to hold lightening in her hand and is spoken of as if she were a goddess. She is indeed "the original godlike creator of the island" (Harris 69). Sapphira convinced her master (Bascomb Wade) to deed the island (a mythical place near South Carolina called Willow Springs) to her and her offspring. She had seven sons by Bascomb then killed him and flew back to Africa. The example of Sapphira Wade draws "upon a notion of inequality in slave culture (the enslaved black woman had no power over her master) [. . .and the] efforts of the seemingly powerless against the seemingly powerful.[. . .] Sapphira Wade's success becomes a historical rewriting in the minds of the hearers" (Harris 59). Although unable to call her ancestor's name, Mama Day is heir to Sapphira's power, supernatural abilities that enable Mama Day to help people on the island. Like Sapphira, Mama Day can also control lightening and one day brings down lightening on Ruby's house because Ruby tried to kill Cocoa. Cocoa's dormant gifts are comparable to those of Mama Day as evidenced at the end of the novel in her ability to communicate with her dead ancestors and husband.

In *Daughters of the Dust: A Novel*, Elizabeth Ayodele[3] Peazant (Eula and Eli's oldest daughter)[4] inherits her special power and insights from Nana Peazant, the elder who had previously called on the dead ancestors to send Unborn Child as a messenger to help heal the rifts in the family. Nana Peazant, the great-grandmother and legend, taught Elizabeth to make protection charms from various items on the island including roots, herbs, flowers, and porcupine quills. Similarly, Anyanwu (whose name means *the sun*) in *Wildseed*, inherits her extranatural abilities from a female ancestor (in this case her mother), and she is a healer. However, Anyanwu is about 300 years old, a shape shifter with the ability to change into any animal or human form, and a priestess, an oracle to the Igbo people in West Africa. Anyanwu's mother made magic. Her mother's dreams were accurate and prophetic. She was also a healer, telepathic, and wealthy. Anyanwu and her mother shared telepathic abilities even from a distance.

This motif of the female African ancestor passing down supernatural power to future generations signifies on the idea in traditional beliefs in many West African cultures that supernatural power is inherited from women. It was from Du Kamisa[5] (a great sorceress), for example, that Sugulun Konde, Son-Jara's[6] mother, inherited her supernatural powers, and therefore her daughter (Sugulun Kulunkan) was also heir to them. Hence, Son-Jara was surrounded by great powers. Sugulun Konde, who is also a healer, initiated her children into the secrets of nature. Son-Jara's success was largely due to the supernatural powers of his mother and sister.

Similar to Du Kamisa, Kassaye (Askia Mohammed's[7] mother) was endowed with great magical powers. "Today a woman by the same name or title reigns in Wanzerbe as the most powerful sorceress of the region" (Hale "Introduction" 11). Kassaye saved her son Mamar Kassaye (Askia Mohammed) from her brother Si (who was told by the seers that Kassaye's child would kill Si and take over the throne of Gao).[8] Kassaye helped her son and was a source of supernatural power for him. Like Son-Jara, Askia's success was due largely to the supernatural power of his mother. In *The Epic of Almami Samori Toure*, one-breasted Demba (Keba's, the King of Sikasso, sister), whose physical deformity signified special power, would no doubt also pass on her powers to her descendants. Demba organized the battle at Woyowayanko in the Manden.

Eve's Bayou, Mama Day, Daughters of the Dust: A Novel, and *Wildseed* reflect traditional West African beliefs about women, as well as problematize Eurocentric notions about women. Far from being weak and passive, the women of African descent in these texts are represented as embodiments of supernatural power, seers, healers, keepers of the oral tradition, and some even control nature. These works project images that reinforce links with Africa and represent continuity within history rather than a rupture between the people and their origin.

Grassroots & Professional Storytellers:
The Fireplace, the Porch, the Stage

Probably the earliest record of a Black woman storyteller and orator in a public arena in North America is that of Lucy Terry (1730-1821), a former slave whose husband (Abijah Prince) bought her freedom. Although remembered today primarily as the first African American to compose poetry (her only extant poem, "Bars Fight" 1746, was recited or sung by Terry), she was during her day a noted public speaker and gained a reputation as an impressive storyteller. Young people often gathered at her house to listen to her stories. She also "once used her eloquence in a three-hour attempt to persuade the Board of Trustees of Williams College to remove the color bar and permit her son to enter the school. On another occasion she brought a suit against Colonel Eli Bronson, her neighbor in Sunberland, Vermont, to the Supreme Court of the United States" (Dannett 30). Dissatisfied with the way her lawyer Isaac Ticknor was representing her case, she argued it for herself before the Supreme Court. "Later, Justice Samuel Chase, who presided, remarked that Lucy's plea 'surpassed that of any Vermont lawyer' he had ever heard" (Dannett 30-31).

Because of the work of Jarena Lee (1783-?), the pulpit in the African Methodist Episcopal (A.M.E.) Church is also a historical, as well as contemporary site, where Black women through preaching preserve and transform the African American oral tradition. In 1818, Lee became the first female preacher of the first A.M.E. Church. By challenging the conservative sex biases of the church, Lee opened the door for herself, as well as for numerous women after her, to walk through and enter the ministry of the A.M.E. Church. When Reverend Richard Williams "lost the spirit" during a sermon he was giving in 1818 at Bethel A.M.E. Church in Philadelphia, Lee "by altogether supernatural impulse" jumped to her feet and gave an inspired exhortation (Lee 513). She recalled, "God made manifest his power in a manner sufficient to show the world that I was called to labor according to my ability" (513). Bishop Richard Allen (of the A.M.E. Church) sanctioned Lee's right to preach as a result of Lee's sermon.[9]

The history of most Black women storytellers and oral historians remains primarily a memory of an elder. In slave narratives, collections of folklore, and various oral history projects about slavery, the narrators often remember a female elder telling them stories and teaching them family history and African traditions. In other cases, however, Black women recorded their own deeds and in that way became storytellers for their own narratives, as well as for others whose stories are incorporated into the "master" narrative which deals with the actions of the female subject. A recurring theme in these chronicles is the dual activity of the Black women--their action and the telling of the deeds. Many of these women went to great lengths to tell and/or record their stories. The most common double action is escape from slavery and the recording of the journey--examples include the stories of Sarah Jane Giddings, Katy, and Harriet Jacobs. Sarah Jane Giddings was a free-born Black woman who was taken to Texas when she was twelve years old and made a slave. She spent ten years as a slave then escaped to Canada. Later, her story was recorded and published.[10]

Katy led her family to freedom then told her story to someone who recorded and published it. The following story and quotations about Katy are from "A Story of the Underground Railroad" (*Douglass' Monthly* January 1859). After Katy witnessed her master whip her husband to death, she was determined to gain her freedom, as well as that of her two daughters (aged ten and twelve at the time of her husband's murder). Twenty years had passed before Katy was able to save enough money to escape the South. By which time, her daughters were married to fellow slaves and each had three children:

> [Katy] felt that she could easily provide for her own safety in flight, but was resolved to leave neither child nor grandchild in bondage. She saw, too, that those incumbrances were increasing in number, that her master was becoming embarrassed in his finances, and that some of them must be sold to relieve him. It might be her own offspring who would thus be taken. While they were united was therefore the time for them to fly. The flight agreed upon, preparation was made, and a night selected. They knew that dogs might be put on their trail. To prevent their feet depositing a scent which the dogs would recognize and follow, they filled their shoes with a preparation which effectively throws them off. [. . .] An hour before midnight the whole party, one daughter alone excepted [who was too afraid to leave], took up their dangerous march.

During their journey toward freedom, they had to hide in swamps or thickets in the daytime. Katy "forded creeks with heavy child on her shoulder, and swam broad rivers, supporting with one hand the same laborious burden." After traveling about four weeks, they encountered a white man ("an agent") who ran the first station on the

Underground Railroad. To their pleasant surprise, they had reached Pennsylvania. The agent gave them food, clean clothes, and a place to sleep. The following night the agent's sons took Katy and her family to Philadelphia. Katy was hired as a cook for a hotel. After saving her wages for three months, she quit her job and returned to Virginia to rescue the daughter who was too afraid to leave the first time. She made her way back to the plantation, and the slaves

> related to her how exasperated her master had been on discovering that ten of his chattels had gone off in a body; that when pursuit had been found unavailing, her poor timid daughter had been subjected to repeated torture to compel a disclosure of the plot; that from this cruelty she was even scarcely recovered; that in the interval the master had died, and that his negroes were all soon to be sold at auction.

The slaves brought Katy's daughter to her, and the two were ready to leave the plantation before midnight. Two men who were "glowing with aspirations for liberty" joined Katy. Following nearly the same route that she had taken during the first escape, Katy again reached the first station on the Underground Railroad in Pennsylvania where the agent gave them food and clothing. The fugitives safely reached freedom.

Harriet Jacobs, after about seven years of hiding, escaped and wrote a book-length narrative about her life as a slave and eventual escape. By the end of that narrative, Jacobs becomes the storyteller/elder for her daughter to whom Jacobs tells her story, an image that is brilliantly re-created in *Beloved* and *Praisesong for the Widow*. At Beloved's request, Sethe recounts a narrative about her mother. Sethe only saw her mother a few times in the fields and once working indigo. She vividly remembers the day her mother showed her a circle and a cross that was burned into the skin of her rib (Morrison 61). Sethe would know her by that mark, she said. One day the slave master hung her mother; Sethe never knew why, but there were numerous enslaved Africans hung that day. The implication is that they were involved in a slave revolt. Although Sethe looked for the mark on her mother's body, she was unable to find it. This painful, traumatic memory halts the story. The image of a female elder passing on history to a female child is also captured in *Praisesong for the Widow*. Aunt Cuney and Avey walk to Ibo Landing, and Aunt Cuney tells Avey the story that her grandmother told her—that of Ibo Landing, the place where the Igbos walked on water back to Africa.

Aunt Cuney's grandmother used to say that her body was in Tatem, but her mind was with the Igbos (Marshall 39). This narrative symbolizes freedom, as well as connects enslaved Africans and their descendants to their origin, Africa (which is the destination of the Igbos in the narrative).

The majority of the grassroots storytellers who captivated audiences by the fireplace and on the porch (the traditional sites of the telling) remain unknown. However, "the power of the front porch has always been a significant part of African American heritage. It was especially significant in the socialization of black children" (Johnson-Coleman 175). From many southern porches "creativity has come historically as well as those specific to Hurston's works. Joe Clarke's storefront in *Their Eyes Were Watching God* (1937), for example, is a famous and creative space. There people observe the world and offer their narrative contributions to it in the form of folktales" (Harris 63-64). *Eve's Bayou* reminds the viewer that the porch was also a place to pass on life lessons as evidenced in the scene when Mozelle joins Eve on the porch after Louis takes Cisely to Roz's mother's house. Mozelle explains that most people experience great pain and loss in life, but there must be a divine point to life which will one day become clear. By the end of the film, Eve learns the truth of Mozelle's words, for Eve does indeed feel terrible pain connected to her father's death and the events that led to his death.

Although relatively little is written about grassroots and professional storytellers, some sources provide insight into the subject. Janie Hunter (who was a professional storyteller), for instance, remembered that when she was a child her parents taught her games, riddles, stories, and folktales; they also taught Hunter "songs from the life of our people in Africa and during slavery" (Hunter 322). After the children cut the wood and wrapped the house with green oak and muckle wood, they would gather by the fire and listen to their parents' stories. As a professional storyteller, Hunter traveled throughout the United States performing. At home, she taught her children stories, songs, and family history; she wanted them to continue the traditions (Carawan 54).

Jennye Dudley remembered childhood years spent huddled with her mother and aunt around the fireplace:

> These moments, those songs should not have been forgotten. The lyrics of those voices cannot be hushed. Her memory conjures the lyrics of haunting slave song. (Daise 49)

A fireplace at night was also "a probable site for reliving local ghost tales. One tale was of 'the hag,' which supposedly sat on people's faces at night as they slept, disorienting and terrorizing them" (Daise 49). Like Dudley's mother and aunt, Miss Deeley chose the fireplace as the cite of storytelling sessions. After dinner was served, she entertained everyone for hours until the children fell asleep:

> After poking around in the fire until she was satisfied that it was burning well, she would lean back in her chair, take a couple of good bites of tobacco, kept in her apron pocket, and then lift up the youngest child into her lap and begin to reminisce about happenings during the day. She had the ability to tell a range of stories, but she seemed particularly adept at hag, ghost, or other psychological thrillers. [. . .] Her subject matter may have been inspired by the proximity of a graveyard to her home; her belief that she had seen spirits of people buried there perhaps added realism to her tales both in her mind and in her listeners' minds. (Jones-Jackson 55-56)

Miss Deeley included songs in some of the tales she told. She was able to create suspense "through an aura of intense dread and to communicate fear and even terror to listeners" (Jones-Jackson 56).

The stage (in the broadest sense of places to perform--from libraries, conferences, and theaters to universities, bookstores, and festivals) is another arena where Black women preserve and transform the oral tradition. The Gullah Festival in Beaufort, South Carolina, for example, features African American professional storytellers each year.[11] Many of these performers learned the significance of and their love for the oral tradition from their parents and grandparents. The primary goals of the Gullah Festival are to promote and preserve an understanding and awareness of African American culture and heritage.

The Hallelujah Singers, a group of 41 people founded by Marlena Smalls (Director) and Anita Singleton-Prather (former Assistant Director and narrator) who are dedicated to preserving Gullah culture, have been performing for packed audiences since 1990 when the group was founded. Most of their material is based on stories passed down from relatives, as well as narratives from the members' own experiences. For example, one narrative is based on Smalls's uncle who went out for revival without an escort and lost his way back home; when they found him, he explained that the devil removed the road signs *(Voices of the Gullah Culture)*. Awards that the Hallelujah Singers have won include the South Carolina Folk

Heritage Advocacy Award, Ambassador Tourism Award 1998 State of South Carolina, and Mayor's Award Key to the City of Rockford (Rockford, Illinois). In 1993, the Hallelujah Singers performed at the Humanities Councils Annual Congregation Breakfast in Washington, D.C. In 1998, the Hallelujah Singers mesmerized audiences at Spoleto USA, the largest festival in the United States and the second largest in the world. The group has also performed before national figures such as Maya Angelou, Marian Wright Edelman, and Hillary Rodham Clinton.

Fouche Sheppard is also an award winning professional storyteller who is dedicated to preserving the African American oral tradition. She is also the Chair of MOJA (an art organization that co-sponsors the MOJA Arts Festival in Charleston). She was born in Charleston, South Carolina and learned stories from her grandmother, Evelina Sheppard, who was a child during the Civil War. Sheppard recalled that her grandmother "just loved using stories particularly the animal stories where the smaller animals outsmarted the larger ones." Sheppard's stories give encouragement and support and her goal is that the audience will learn that "there is a solution to every problem. *Even an ant can eat a mountain.*" (Grayson, "A Conversation with Fouche Sheppard")

Although *Eve's Bayou* captures the motif of Black women as preservers of the oral tradition, that history remains to be told. One of the major difficulties of such a project is that most of the history of Black women storytellers was not recorded. However, contemporary storytellers who continue the tradition keep the narratives alive, and parts of the past can be traced by recording the stories of women who learned the art of the oral tradition from their mothers and grandmothers who, in turn, were trained by their elders and back through the generations to the origin in West African nations. To conclude this chapter and provide an example of the rich material that Black women storytellers preserve, I included my complete interview with Fouche Sheppard.

* * * * *

**A Conversation with Fouche Sheppard,
Professional Storyteller[12]**

**Grayson: Your mother plays an important part in your life.
How would you describe her?**
Sheppard: My mother, Viola Gathers, is 89 years old. We live
together. At one time, she was a pastry chef then a domestic worker.
She would take my siblings and I with her to work because she did
not have anyone to watch us. In her later life, she was a grounds
keeper and retired in that position for a local cemetery at 84 years old.
She is very active, and she works very closely with me. She taught
herself to read the Bible when she was 69 years old because she
wanted develop her own relationship with God; she can read and
comprehend everything. She opens for me sometimes. The last time
she opened for me was in 1996 when I was featured in the SPOLETO
Festival in Charleston. I always put her on the spot and ask her to do
or say something before I perform because what I do in my art form
is what my grandmother (Evelina Sheppard) taught me, and my
grandfather (Daniel Sheppard) taught her. My mother is an excellent
vocalist. She would sing these songs that my grandfather sang when
he was burdened down such as "Loose The Man:"

> Oh Satan loose the man
> and let him go.
> You can't do nothing til you loose the man
> and let him go.

My grandfather sang all of the songs in full verse, and my
grandmother taught me all of the stanzas of the spirituals.
**Grayson: What is an example of a story about slavery that you
learned from your family?**
Sheppard: My grandmother, who was a child during the Civil War,
told me that when she was very young on the plantation, the Yankee
soldiers were supposed to be coming to help African Americans.
However, all of the children actually had to hide from the soldiers
because the Yankees would steal the children and sell them down in
Louisiana or someplace else even though they were free in South
Carolina. She would only tell stories about slavery on special
occasions, especially if she wanted to get a point across to me about
human nature. It was very painful for her to tell those stories because
she would start to remember and sometimes tears would roll down
her cheeks.

**Grayson: How did your grandmother feel about the Gullah and
English languages?**
Sheppard: My grandmother felt that white people talk was an
invasion of privacy in her home, so she did not want me speaking
English. However, she wanted me to be able to read the Bible to her.
I think it was her way of training me and conditioning me as a child.
She used the book of Psalms and the book of Proverbs as a guideline
for how I should behave. I remember as a teenager when I wanted to
do something that she might not necessarily approve of she would
say, "What God say?" She knew that I knew because for years I had
been reading the words to her. After I got through reading a chapter
of the Bible to her, she would ask me, "You know what that mean?" If
I told her "yes," she would say, "You know; you really know?"
    "Yes ma'am."
    "Well if you know and you don't do, then God gonna get you."
    She taught me to have an intimate relationship with God on a
spiritual level. She had a fear of God built up in me. As a child, I did
not want to do anything that God would not like. You could not have
any hatred in your heart. You had to want the highest and best for
everyone. If I did not understand a Bible passage, she would explain
it to me. She also taught me by using Gullah proverbs. If I had been
excluded from something, for example, she would say, "You never
see eagles fly with other birds because eagles don't fly in flocks." She
wanted me to feel special.
    My third grade teacher was teaching me to read the Bible so that I
could read to my grandmother, but I could not talk that white people
talk in my grandmother's house because that was *she house. She
done been in the white people house all day* so that meant I had to
speak Gullah in her house. It worked very well for us. It helped us to
have a very intimate relationship. She also taught me to dance. She
was an excellent tap dancer and would talk me through a dance-- that
is how I learned.
    My grandmother was never afraid of white people, and she always
told me to look them in their eyes. She also believed in the virtuous
woman. To her, the virtuous woman was responsible, the head of the
household who made sure that the family was taken care of, and the
one person God could use. The virtuous woman was a warrior as well
as a nurturer. She had to be the one to keep things together no matter
how painful it was for her. I see the pattern in my mother also. My
grandmother never remarried, and I never got into other relationships
after my divorce. My grandmother contributed to that because she

told me I had a child to raise, and I couldn't *go from man to man like a dollar bill go from hand to hand cause I got a girl child.* Those kinds of things kept me in check. I had to get an education, so I could teach the child the way to go, and *God will show the child the way for go.*

Grayson: What are some of the special burial rituals that your family practiced?
Sheppard: During my early years when people in the community died, they had the wake in the home. When my stepfather died on September 10, 1960, his body was laid in the living room the night before the funeral. People would come in and pay tribute. Most of the people when they paid tribute would put a few dollars in my mother's hand in addition to bringing food. It was understood that the money was to help with the funeral expenses.

If there are any young children (five years old and younger) at the burial ground when the love one is laid to rest, the children are passed over the coffin. One person would stand on one side of the coffin and pass the child over to someone else who would receive the child on the other side. This practice keeps the spirit from coming back to haunt the child, especially if the child had a close relationship with the person. Everyone danced [sacred dance] at the funeral. When the body is being placed into the ground, people sing (usually an upbeat song). "Uncloudy Day" is one of the main songs.

The lid was open by the grave, so you could see the person. The lid was placed on the coffin just before it was placed in the ground. You had a final viewing and sometimes that gave people the opportunity to put flowers (or whatever they wanted to put) with the body. My mom put my stepfather's wedding band, watch, and hat back on him. They also talk with the person. Another tradition is that a lot of people still kiss the dead person in the coffin just before they bury him as an expression of their love and loyalty.

Grayson: What are examples of signs that indicate that a child has supernatural powers?
Sheppard: If a child was born with the foot foremost or a veil over her/his eyes, the child has special powers. Also if the child was the seventh child, particularly a female, then she was supposed to be endowed spiritually and trained spiritually. Usually, the elder of the community would train that child. I think that was why it went from my grandmother to me. My mother guided me, but my relationship with my mother was not as intimate as that with my grandmother.

Grayson: Who was the primary person from whom you learned stories?

Sheppard: My grandmother. She just loved using stories particularly the animal stories where the smaller animals outsmarted the larger ones. My grandmother also taught me about performing and being able to express myself. I think everything I am now is everything my grandmother wanted to be but couldn't realize in her lifetime.

Grayson: What is your favorite animal story?

Sheppard: "The Signifying Monkey" because that is the first story that my grandmother taught me:

The lion just got done eating a great big antelope, and he was thinking with this last piece he threw in his mouth, "I think I'll take me a nap." The monkey, who was flying around in a tree as the lion was beating on his belly, looked down and said, "Mr. Lion, Mr. Lion, I got something to tell you." [The lion ignored the monkey.] The monkey looked down at the lion very upset and started to swing in the trees: "Who does that lion think he is? I want to talk to him, and he don't want to talk to me." The monkey was swinging through the trees and all of a sudden he came to a clearing. In the clearing, there was an elephant. The elephant had just got done eating a big bag of peanuts. He had one more in his trunk to throw into his mouth, and he dropped it on the ground. He said, "I think I am going to take me a nap."

The monkey looked down at the elephant and started to swing. He said, "If I could get that lion and that elephant to fight that would be the biggest fight. Gotta be something I could do. I know." The monkey turned around and started swinging back to the lion. "Mr. Lion, Mr. Lion. I got something to tell you. There is a great big elephant down the way talk about your mama in a scandalous way." The lion opened his eyes wide. "Uh huh. Talked about your mama and your grandmama too and ain't said nothing nice about you." The lion jumped up on his feet. The monkey had him then, "What he said about your mama sure nough made me mad."

The lion replied, "Oh yeah? I'll fix him. I'll tear that elephant limb from limb." The lion took off with a mighty roar (sounded like a shot from a forty four) and came up on the elephant where the tall grass grows. The elephant looked at the lion, "What? You best go pick on somebody your own size." The lion did not listen; he made a pass. The elephant knocked him to the grass. Mr. Lion jumped up with a mighty sound that's when the elephant really went to town. He whipped that lion all that day. I still don't know how that lion got away. Got away he did more dead than alive and that's when that monkey started his signifyin jive. The monkey looked down laughing, "Is that you Mr. Lion? He whipped you good." The monkey was laughing jumping up and down. Feet missed a limb, and he fell to the ground. Then the lion was on that monkey with all four feet. He was going to grind that monkey into hamburger meat, but the monkey looked up with tears in his eyes, "Please, please, Mr. Lion. I apologize. I didn't mean any harm. Please let me go, and I'll tell you something you really need to know." Lion stepped back to hear what he had to say, that slick old Monkey scampered up the tree and got away. "What I wanted to tell you," he said, "is that if you mess with me I'll get that elephant on you again." The lion looked up and said, "If you want to stay alive, up in that tree you better stay." That my friends is where we find all those signifying monkeys to this very day.

My grandmother used that story for several reasons: 1) You never want to go jump up into somebody's face without giving the person a chance to explain the situation because you never know what kind of weapon the person may have. 2) It is easy to get in trouble, but it is so hard to get out. 3) The monkey, the smallest animal, used his brain and outwitted the two larger animals and then he got away clean. My grandmother would use this story in different ways, but the first time she told it to me was because as a child I had gotten into a fight with someone who talked about my mother.

Grayson: What is your most memorable experience performing?
Sheppard: My very first performance for the MOJA Arts Festival in 1985. A dear friend of mine who was familiar with me doing poetry tricked me into performing for MOJA. He called me two hours before I was to be on stage and told me the people were looking for me to be at the Garden Theater. When I got on that stage and presented some poems, the people in the community applauded. They let me know afterward how much they loved it. Another memorable event was my first theater experience which was with MOJA in the 90s. I performed in *One Monkey Don't Stop No Show*. I was the only cast member who spoke Gullah. I acted just like a Gullah mother would act. That was also a good experience because of the excellent response after the performance.

Grayson: What are some of the major differences between performing as a professional storyteller and private storytelling?
Sheppard: Private storytelling allows you the opportunity to dig deep within your soul--to do soul searching and to express feelings that you need to be able to express openly. It also allows you to set your emotions free. Public storytelling broadens storytelling in that you are able to reach others, especially youth. You can also make a difference in people's lives by telling stories of hope. Storytelling is very rewarding and enriching, especially when passed down from one generation to the next. Both forms are very important. The stories entertain, as well as provide insight that people can use for the rest of their lives.

Grayson: What do you hope people will learn from your stories?
Sheppard: That you are very important. There is a purpose in life, and it is up to you to find your purpose. God wants you to know what that purpose is, but you have to desire life for yourself. Nobody else can do that but you. The stories give encouragement and positive support. They show something about human nature, as well as how to overcome problems. There is a solution to every problem. *Even an ant can eat a mountain.* You will be able to accomplish your goals regardless of what anyone else says. You can go after something, be determined, and persevere.

Notes

[1]Although this story of Eve is fictional, in the 18th century there was an enslaved African woman in Louisiana who had borne 10 children for her master (a French planter), and although not a common practice, he willed his land to her.
[2]Like Mozelle, Eve discovers that she has the power of sight when she is ten years old.
[3]Ayodele was the first Peazant to walk on the Sea Island. Elizabeth is the first daughter of the first son and for this reason has the name Ayodele which means "her who brings joy." Ayodele came into the world hand first which is a good sign and a symbol that she would bring prosperity (Dash, *Daughters of the Dust: A Novel* 87).
[4]The Unborn Child in the film *Daughters of the Dust* grows up to be Elizabeth in the novel.

[5]Du Kamisa is also a shape-shifter. After her nephew, the new king, excludes her from the family, she transforms herself into a buffalo and kills men in the Manden. (Sisoko, *The Epic of Son-Jara*)

[6]Son-Jara was the founder of the Empire of Old Mali (13th century).

[7]Askia Mohammed was the most famous leader in the history of the Songhay Empire. He reigned from 1493 to 1528.

[8]Si killed seven of Kassaye's children. Later, she was pregnant with the child of a djin (spirit and the chief of the city under the river). She saved her child (Askia Mohammed) by switching him with the female child of a slave. Si blessed the boy but killed the female child who he believed to be Kassaye's child. Askia Mohammed became the servant of his uncle. When Askia learned the truth of his ancestry, he killed Si. (Hale, *The Epic of Askia Mohammed*)

[9]When Lee had first approached then Reverend Allen eight years earlier after she was moved by a vision to preach, he told her that his discipline did not call for women preachers, but she could hold prayer meetings. Reflecting on Allen's decision, Lee later wrote, "Why should it be thought impossible, heterodox, or improper for a woman to preach? Seeing the Saviour died for the woman as well as for the man. [. . .] Did not Mary *first* preach the risen Saviour, and is not the doctrine of the resurrection the very climax of Christianity--hangs not all our hope on this, as argued by St. Paul? Then did not Mary, a woman, preach the gospel? For she preached the resurrection of the crucified Son of God" (511).

[10]This information about Giddings is from an untitled article in *Douglass' Monthly* October 1859. Originally titled *North Star* (1847), *Douglass' Monthly* was established by Frederick Douglass and became one of the leading abolitionist newspapers of the era. In the inaugural edition of the *North Star*, Douglass dedicated his newspaper "to the cause of our long oppressed and plundered fellow countryman" and announced that the newspaper "shall fearlessly assert your rights, faithfully proclaim your wrongs, and earnestly demand for you instant and even-handed justice. Giving no quarter to slavery at the South, it will hold no truce with oppressors at the North. While it shall boldly advocate emancipation for our enslaved brethren, it will omit no opportunity to gain for the nominally free, complete enfranchisement" (Douglass, "Editorial in the Inaugural Edition of the *North Star*" 124).

[11]The Gullah Festival also includes lectures, historical exhibits, fine arts and historical displays, Gullah presentations, music, and the Black Inventions Museum.

[12]I conducted this interview in January 1999 at the Avery Research Center for African American History and Culture in Charleston, South Carolina. An audio version (which includes stories, proverbs, and poems in Gullah) is available through the Avery Research Center for African American History and Culture. This interview was originally published in *Network 2000: In the Spirit of the Harlem Renaissance* (6.2 Spring 1999) and is part of my oral

history project titled "Speaking and Singing the Narrative: An Introduction to Black Women Storytellers in Low Country South Carolina." Special thanks to Sherman E. Pyatt (Archivist, Avery Research Center) for his assistance with this interview.

Chapter 6

Looking Back with Scholarly Eyes

Central to *Sankofa, Daughters of the Dust*, and *Eve's Bayou* are the subject positions of Black women who are represented in a variety of roles including warriors, educators, healers, seers, keepers of the oral tradition, as well as mothers, sisters, daughters, and wives. Essential to these films is precisely what is erased in society, for despite the fact that Black women were active agents in shaping their own lives as well as altering the course of history, their roles in world history are generally overlooked and/or dismissed--oversights which can be considered suppression through historical omission. Examples of information that is usually ignored include the ways that Black women resisted slavery in North America and Black women entrepreneurs who sought their economic independence in a hostile slave society, subjects on which this chapter focuses.

One of the ways that Black women resisted slavery was through revolts. For example, at least one Black woman was involved in a slave revolt in New York in 1712; after the revolt, twenty one slaves were executed, "one being a woman with child, her execution by that means suspended" ("Report of Governor Hunter"). In August 1829, a Black woman, also unnamed, was one of six leaders who planned to kill the traders leading them from Maryland to the South to be sold. Two white people, the leader and a guard, were killed and most of the slaves escaped. However, a posse captured the slaves and all six leaders were sentenced to be hung. On November 20, 1829, the five men were hanged. Because "the woman was found to be pregnant [she was] permitted to remain in jail for several months until after the birth of the child, whereupon, on May 25, 1830, she was publicly hanged" (Aptheker 287). Black women were also involved in fights with the militia. In South Carolina, for instance, a Black woman and a child (both fugitives) were killed during a confrontation between a body of militia and a community of fugitive slaves (Aptheker 277). In other cases, a woman would "rebel in a manner commensurate with the work demands imposed upon her. 'She'd get stubborn like a mule and quit,'" or she would take her hoe, knock down the overseer, and hit him across the head (Jones 21).

Another form of resistance was to poison the master. Many Black women had "knowledge of and access to poisonous herbs, gleaned from African as well as Indian and other American lore, which they transmitted down through the generations" (Fox-Genovese 306). White residents of South Carolina were so concerned about this issue that in 1751 they amended the Negro Act of 1740 as follows:

> Any black who should instruct another "in the knowledge of any poisonous root, plant, herb, or other poison whatever, he or she, so offending shall upon conviction thereof suffer death as a felon." The law also prohibited physicians, apothecaries, or druggists from admitting slaves to places in which drugs were kept or allowing them to administer drugs to other slaves. (Fox-Genovese 306)

Moreover, in 1811, Kentucky "declared conspiracy or poisoning by slaves, crimes punishable by death" (Aptheker 261). It is unclear how many Black women poisoned their masters, but as cooks and house servants, the women were in a strategic position to do so. Black women also protested slavery through narratives, poetry, speeches, essays, and fiction. Furthermore, between the 1830s and the 1840s, they were among the twenty to thirty thousand slaves who escaped the South. Black women were also among an estimated fifty thousand fugitives living in Canada in 1855.

Black women also actively sought their economic independence during the antebellum period (an action which can also be seen as a form of resisting slavery). Many nineteenth century paintings and sketches of the antebellum period re-create scenes of Black women entrepreneurs who sought their economic independence in a hostile slave society. Rose Nicaud's coffee stand (represented in the painting "Rose Nicaud's Coffee Stand in French Quarter")[1] and Black women street vendors in South Carolina (illustrated in nineteenth century newspapers and magazines) give insight into two of the methods (coffee stands and vending goods such as fruit and vegetables) through which women of African descent actively sought their physical and economic liberation in a racist and sexist slave society-- a brutal society in which freedom and equal rights were denied Black people. Antebellum Black women entrepreneurs, most of whose names have been lost, were part of a tradition that is generally overlooked and/or ignored but has been visually recorded in paintings and sketches.

The painting "Rose Nicaud's Coffee Stand in French Quarter" is attributed to the artist Richard Clague[2] (1821-1873) and estimated to have been painted in the mid-1800s (probably when Clague was in New Orleans in 1857). The piece is an image of Rose Nicaud at her business, a coffee stand in the French Quarter in New Orleans. Nicaud was born a slave[3] in New Orleans and later bought her freedom through "thrift and economy and lived to a ripe old age" ("Street Vendors and Street Cries" 7). In the painting, Rose Nicaud (wearing a long dress and an apron) is in front of the counter of her business carrying a cup of coffee to a customer, a man wearing a hat and suit who is seated on a stool. A second man (also a customer and wearing a hat and suit) is seated near the first. The second man is facing the counter so the viewer cannot see his face, but his elbow and hand are lifted in a position that indicate he is drinking a cup of coffee. A third man (apparently not a customer) is on the opposite side of coffee stand walking past the two customers.

Black women owned most of the coffee stands scattered over old New Orleans and the French Market. The most famous coffee stall in the French Market was that of Rose Nicaud. She also had the most "cosmopolitan spot in New Orleans, attracting wealthy planters as well as men from the luggers, who couldn't start their day without a cup of Rose's cafe au lait" (Roehl). Since she ran a coffee house in the French Quarter, she would have had to obtain a license from the city to operate the business. "Beginning in 1814 the City Council implemented regulations setting forth the obligations of licenses and requiring that they subscribe 'jointly and severally with another solvent person to the satisfaction of the mayor,' security bonds for the proper execution of those obligations. The amount of the bond varied according to the purpose or occupation being licensed."[4] In the 1840s, a security bond for a coffee house was about one thousand dollars.

On a typical day, Rose Nicaud's street cry of "Cafe noir!" or "Cafe au lait!" would blend with the cries of slave vegetable vendors. One of her customers said that her coffee was "like the benediction that follows after prayer; or if you prefer it, like the benedictine after dinner" (Cole 22). The process by which she created her famous coffee follows:

> [Rose would] pile the golden powder of ground French Market coffee into her French strainer— a heaping tablespoon for each cup--and then when the pot was well heated, pour in just two tablespoons, no more, of boiling water. In ten minutes this had soaked the coffee, and then, half a cup at a time, the boiling water poured on and allowed to drip slowly. The result would be coffee, black, clear and sparkling--ideal French Market coffee. (Cole 22)

A watercolor sketch by Leon Fremaux provides a clue to the exact dates of Rose Nicaud's coffee stand. In the sketch, Rose (wearing a long dress and an apron) is pictured standing in front of the counter of her business. She looks older than in the Clague painting of the 1850s. She is pouring coffee into a cup. The caption reads "Rose, who sells coffee in the French Market." Fremaux credited Nicaud with showing him the different types of tignon coiffures and noted that she was known to the "entire French and Creole population" and "for thirty-five years had sold bread and coffee" at the French Market (39). The sketch was probably drawn during the 1870s (and published in 1876 with other watercolors). Using 1876 as the date of Fremaux's sketch of Rose Nicaud at her coffee stand and the 35 year marker he gave in relation to her coffee business, Nicaud probably opened her coffee stand around 1841 and her business continued to prosper beyond 1876.

Referred to in *Frank Leslie's Illustrated Newspaper* as an "institution," the Charleston Black street vendors were a major part of the city. A visual record of this "institution" is accessible through newspapers, magazines, and archival collections including *Frank Leslie's Illustrated, Harper's Weekly, The Illustrated London News, Picturesque America,* and the Black Charleston and Slavery and Freedom Collection at the Avery Research Center for African American History and Culture. During the antebellum period, slave vendors sold goods for their masters and the profit had to be given to the slave owner. Some enslaved Africans, however, were able to save some of the profit, and through many, many years of saving were able to buy their freedom and later that of their family members. Street vending was also an avenue for Blacks (free and slave) to provide for themselves and their families. Usually carrying a broad basket on their heads, in the traditional African manner, containing the items for sale (fruit, vegetables, fish, or other items), the street vendors announced their presence and goods available through a variety of rhythmical and musical cries describing the items for sale. Examples of street cries include:

- Coming on a Tuesday morning Raw! Raw! Raw! Shrimp
- Monkey meat [5] and ground-nut cake [6].
  Come on children get your monkey meat.
- Red Rose Tomatoes.
- Strawberry. Fresh and fine and just off the vine. Strawberry.
- Load my Gun, With sweet sugar plum, And shoot them nung gal, one by one, Barder lingo, Watermelon.
- Old Joe Cole-Good old Soul, Porgy in the Summer-time, And Whiting in the Spring, 8 upon a string, Don't be late I'm waiting at the gate, Don't be mad-Here's your shad, Old Joe Cole-Good Old Soul.
- Porgy walk, Porgy talk, Porgy eat with a knife and fork. She crab, She crab. [7]

Some religious vendors might combine the selling of their goods with a scripture lesson. [8] Coming out of African nations that already had an established, successful tradition of trade and city marketing, enslaved and free Blacks excelled in trade in Charleston and other Southern cities (Walker 2).

> The precolonial African propensity for trading and marketing constituted a business ethos, which survived the Atlantic passage and consequently provided a foundation for the origin of the African-American business tradition. [. . .] The historical significance of colonial African-slave economic initiatives is that, notwithstanding their subordinate legal and societal status, enslaved Africans in America forged a business tradition derived initially from their African commercial heritage in trade and marketing. (Walker 2)

Many free Black women who participated in the food services industry (and established food stalls, cookshops, bakeries, confectioneries, restaurants, and catering enterprises) "were initially food vendors who prepared their food at home or at their stalls for sale to a busy urban population" (Walker 135). "The Charleston City directory shows that seven of the nine leading black grocers, fruit dealers, and confectioners were women" (Fitchett 74). Another example of an industry in which many Black women worked was the garment trades. In 1848 in Charleston, for instance, 128 free Black women were mantua-makers,[9] 68 were seamstresses, and 6 were tailors, while 20 enslaved Black women were seamstresses and 36 were tailors (Fitchett 74). Although very few free Black women acquired substantial wealth as businesswomen, the "resolute few who worked for themselves achieved greater earnings than those who worked for others" (Walker 149). In a society that was racist, sexist, as well as "decidedly hostile in its oppression and exploitation of black woman, the economic achievement of black women, both slave and free, through business enterprises that they established, is remarkable" (Walker 149).

After the Civil War and until around the late 1950s, street vending continued to be an avenue through which Blacks could earn money and provide for themselves and their families. Rosa Moore, for example, sent her son through college by selling vegetables. In 1957, Moore was still a familiar face (she had been selling vegetables for 35 years). Her cart was filled with turnips, corn, beans, squash, and other produce that was in season. She won a prize for her song:

> I come all way from Jim Island.
> Yes Ma'am, I got stringbeans
> I got tender okra
> I got peaches
> Peaches. Georrrrrgia peaches.
> Yes, Ma'am. I got vegetable. Fresh vegetable. (Leland 1-C)

Like Moore, Bertha Huggins was still an active vendor in 1957. Huggins had a two-acre farm and was a vendor for over 26 years.

Rose Nicaud's coffee stand and street vendors in antebellum South Carolina give insight into two of the methods that antebellum Black women actively sought their economic liberation in a racist, sexist, and brutal slave society. These female entrepreneurs were part of a tradition that is generally overlooked and/or ignored in historical studies. Through their focus on women of African descent as active agents of change in their own lives and in history, *Sankofa*, *Daughters of the Dust*, and *Eve's Bayou* serve as calls to remember the significant roles of Black women in history, as well as in contemporary society.

Notes

[1] This painting is in storage at the Presbytere Louisiana State Museum.

[2] "Three known paintings by Clague of New Orleans are Rose Nicaud's Coffee Stand at the French Market, Halfway House (location unknown) a famous coffee house on Shell Road near the Metairie Race Course, now Metairie Cemetery, and Treme Market (1863), one of Clague's few watercolors, this is one of his rare dated paintings. It is also one of the very few in which urban architecture is feature. Even so, he included his favorite subjects, water and a bridge, here, a crossing over the Carondelet Canal in Faubourg Treme with the tower of the Treme Market in the center of the painting. Until after the Second World War, each neighborhood had a public market where stalls were rented to butchers, seafood, and vegetable dealers. This watercolor is a rare document of a scene long since gone. The canal which leads from Bayou St. John to Rampart near present Orleans Street has been filled in and the fire two-story hip roof Creole storehouses with deep galleries have been demolished" (Toledano 37).

[3] I speculate that Rose Nicaud was the former slave of Michel Nicaud, a native of Port-du-Paix St. Domingo and his wife De Marguerite Rinchker, a native of Jeremie, St. Domingo. Michel Died Nov. 8, 1840. He was 31 years old. His parents were Michel Desire Nicaud and Dame Marguerite Regnier.

[4] "License Information." New Orleans City Archives Collection (available at the New Orleans Public Library).

[5] Monkey meat is a coconut and molasses candy.

[6] Ground-nut cake is a candy. A recipe for this candy from Gay, Lettie, ed. *200 Years of Charleston Cooking* (New York: Jonathan Cape & Harrison Smith, 1930) follows:

> 1 quart molasses
> 1 cup brown sugar
> ½ cup butter
> 4 cups peanuts, parched and shelled
> Combine the first three ingredients and boil half an hour over a slow fire. Then add the roasted and shelled peanuts and continue cooking for fifteen minutes. Pour into a lightly greased shallow pan and allow to harden. Break into pieces. This makes a somewhat chewy candy similar to taffy.

[7] See "Cries of Charleston" (Available at the Charleston County Library); Leiding, *Street Cries of an Old Southern City*; Hill, "A Remnant of the Past;" Sparkman, "Charleston's Street Vendors;" "Doing the Charleston With His Lordship."

[8] *Harper's Weekly* November 27, 1880.

[9] A mantua-maker is a person who made loose fitting gowns, cloaks, or robes worn in the 17th, 18th, and 19th centuries.

Conclusion

Seeming to respond to Anna Julia Cooper's 1892 call "Only the BLACK WOMAN can say 'when and where I enter [. . .] then and there the whole *Negro race enters with me,*'" *Sankofa*, *Daughters of the Dust*, and *Eve's Bayou* represent Black women as integral to the histories re-created in the films and by extension essential to world history. These narratives are positioned as always already tied to beliefs about and roles of women in traditional West African societies. As extensions of the oral tradition, the texts indicate the relevance of the past to the present and the future.

Sankofa, *Daughters of the Dust*, and *Eve's Bayou* also represent enslaved Africans as asserting themselves through practicing West African traditions, actions that show them as actors in history and independent thinkers. Moreover, the films include new icons to symbolize (and image) the experiences of enslaved Africans and their descendants and the continuation, as well as transformation, of traditional West African beliefs in North America. Using the notion of defamiliarization, the films take everyday animals and objects and present them in unusual ways. A buzzard, for example, is the architect of a spiritual journey in *Sankofa*; hands in *Daughters of the Dust* are stained with indigo dye symbolizing slavery and its impact on enslaved Africans and their descendants--even unborn children; a mirror in *Eve's Bayou* becomes a window into the past, rather than an object that reflects the self. As political films, they serve to redefine Black history and mythic memory in an effort to liberate and decolonize minds.

Unburdened by a linear, progressive construct of history, *Sankofa*, *Daughters of the Dust*, and *Eve's Bayou* utilize the visual and symbolic, as well as oral narratives to represent many of the historical realities of slavery. Furthermore, the films broaden the method of framing history. Rather than using major wars as markers (as is generally the case with traditional American methodology), these films image history through iconography, as well as community-based stories, creating a multi-faceted approach to the subject matter and preserving (and often transforming) the African American oral tradition. By extending the analysis of *Sankofa*, *Daughters of the Dust*, and *Eve's Bayou* into a wider landscape through an examination of the films within African and African American cultural and historical contexts, as well as within an analysis of archival materials, primary and secondary texts, and fieldwork, the stories do more than continue, the codes are deciphered.

Bibliography

Abimbola, Adetokunbo. "Sango Images of an African Empire Builder." *Journal for the Third Millennium* 1 (Spring 1997): 21-24.

Abimbola, Wande. *Ifa: An Exposition of the Ifa Literary Corpus.* Ibadan: Oxford University Press Nigeria, 1976.

---. "Ifa as a Body of Knowledge and as an Academic Corpus." *Journal of Culture and Ideas.* 1 (1983): 1-11.

---. *Sixteen Great Poems of Ifa.* Unesco, 1975.

---. *Ifa Divination Poetry.* New York: Nok Publishers, 1977.

Abiodun, Rowland. "Woman in Yoruba Religious Images." *African Languages and Cultures* 2.1 (1989): 1-18.

Adjei, S.F. Deputy Director of the Centre for National Culture. Personal interview. Kumasi, Ghana West Africa. Summer 1998.

Agyeman-Duah, J., recorder. "Amoaful Stool History." *Ashanti Stool Histories Volume II.* Compiled by K. Ampom Darkwa and B.C. Obaka. University of Ghana, Legon: Institute of African Studies, 1976. Classification Number 200. 1-11.

---, recorder. "Anyinase Stool History." *Ashanti Stool Histories Volume I.* Compiled by K. Ampom Darkwa and B.C. Obaka. University of Ghana, Legon: Institute of African Studies, 1976. Classification Number 78. 1-6.

---, recorder. "Juaben Paramount Stool History." *Ashanti Stool Histories Volume I.* Compiled by K. Ampom Darkwa and B.C. Obaka. University of Ghana, Legon: Institute of African Studies, 1976. Classification Number 16. 1-9.

"The Animal Court." *Tales of the Congaree*. Ed. Robert G. O'Meally. Chapel Hill: University of North Carolina Press, 1987. 63-64.

Aptheker, Herbert. *American Negro Slave Revolts*. New York: International Publishers, 1987.

Badejo, Diedre. *Osun Seegesi: The Elegant Deity of Wealth, Power, and Feminity*. Trenton, New Jersey: Africa World Press, 1996.

Baker, Houston. "Not Without My Daughters: A Conversation with Julie Dash and Houston A. Baker, Jr.," *Transition*. 57 (1992): 150-166.

Bambara, Toni Cade. "Salvation Is The Issue." *Black Women Writers 1950-1980*. Ed. Mari Evans. New York: Doubleday, 1984.

Bascom, William. *Ifa Divination*. Bloomington: Indiana University Press, 1969.

Beier, Ulli. "Gelede Masks." *Odu*. VI (1958): 5-24.

---. *Yoruba Poetry*. Cambridge: Cambridge University Press, 1970.

Boahen, Adu with Jacobs F. Ade and Michael Tidy. *Topics in West African History*. England: Longman Group, 1986.

Bontemps, Arna. *Black Thunder*. Boston: Beacon Press, 1992.

Botkin, B. A., ed. *Lay My Burden Down*. Athens: The University of Georgia Press, 1945.

Bradford, Sarah, ed. *Harriet Tubman: The Moses of Her People*. Secaucus: The Citadel Press, 1961.

Brown, Ann. "Eve's Bayou." *American Visions*.

Butler, Octavia. *Wildseed*. New York: Warner Books, 1980.

Carawan, Guy and Candi. *Ain't You Got A Right to the Tree of Life?: The People of Johns Island, South Carolina: Their Faces, Their Words, and Their Songs*. University of Georgia Press, 1989.

Clarke, John Henrik. "African Warrior Queens." *Black Women in Antiquity*. Ed. Ivan Van Sertima. New Brunswick: Transaction Publishers, 1992. 123-134.

Cole, Catherine. *The Story of the Old French Market*. The New Orleans Coffee Co., 1916

Cooper, Anna Julia. *A Voice from the South*. New York: Oxford University Press, 1988.

"Cries of Charleston." Available at the Charleston County Library.

Curtin, Philip D. *The Atlantic Slave Trade: A Census*. Madison: The University of Wisconsin Press, 1969.

Daise, Donald. *Reminiscences of Sea Island Heritage*. Orangeburg, South Carolina. Sandlapper Publishing, 1986.

Dannett, Sylvia G. L. *Profiles of Negro Womanhood Volume I 1619-1900*. Chicago: Educational Heritage, 1964.

Danquah, Joseph B. *The Akan Doctrine of God.* London: Lutterworth Press, 1944.

Dash, Julie. *Daughters of the Dust: The Making of an African American Woman's Film.* New York City: The New Press, 1992.

---. *Daughters of the Dust: A Novel.* New York: Dutton, 1997.

Daughters of the Dust. Videocassette. Written and Directed by Julie Dash. Geechee Girls Productions, 1991. 113 minutes.

Davis, Angela. *Women, Race, and Class.* New York: Vintage Books, 1983.

"Doing the Charleston With His Lordship." *News and Courier.* April 22, 1959.

Douglass, Frederick. *My Bondage and My Freedom.* New York: Dover Publications, 1969.

---. *Narrative of the Life of Frederick Douglass.* New York: Dolphin Books, 1963.

---. "American Prejudice Against Color: An Address Delivered in Cork, Ireland, 23 October 1845." *The Frederick Douglass Papers Volume 1: 1841-46.* Ed. John W. Blassingame. New Haven: Yale University Press, 1979. 59-70.

---. "America's Compromise with Slavery and the Abolitionists' Work: An Address Delivered in Paisley, Scotland, on 6 April 1846," *The Frederick Douglass Papers Volume 1: 1841-46.* Ed. John W. Blassingame. New Haven: Yale University Press, 1979. 209-215.

---. "American and Scottish Prejudice Against the Slave: An Address Delivered in Edinburgh, Scotland, on 1 May 1846." *The Frederick Douglass Papers Volume 1: 1841-46.* Ed. John W. Blassingame. New Haven: Yale University Press, 1979. 243-249.

---. *The Heroic Slave. Three Classic African-American Novels.* Ed. William L. Andrews New York: Penguin Books, 1990.

---. "Editorial in the Inaugural Edition of the *North Star.*" *The Winding Road to Freedom.* Ed. Alfred E. Cain. Chicago, IL: Educational Heritage, 1965.

Douglass Monthly. October 1859.

Drums and Shadows. Georgia Writer's Project. Athens: The University of Georgia Press, 1986.

Ellison, Ralph. "The Art of Fiction: An Interview." *Shadow and Act.* New York: Random House, 1953.

Eve's Bayou. Videocassette. Written and Directed by Kasi Lemmons. Trimark, 1997.

Fanon, Franz. *The Wretched of the Earth.* New York: Grove Press, 1963.

Farrar, Tarikhu. "The Queen Mother, Matriarchy, and the Question on Female Political Authority in Precolonial West African Monarchy." *Journal of Black Studies* 27.5 (May 1997): 579-597.

Faulkner, William J. *The Days When the Animals Talked*. Trenton: Africa World Press, 1993.

Finnegan, Ruth. *Limba Stories and Story-Telling*. Oxford: Clarendon Press, 1967.

Fitchett, E. Horace. "The Free Negro in Charleston, South Carolina." Diss. University of Chicago, 1950.

Fox-Genovese, Elizabeth. *Within the Plantation Household*. Chapel Hill, NC: The University of North Carolina, 1988.

Fremaux, Leon. *Leon Fremaux's New Orleans Characters*. Ed. Patrick J. Geary. Gretna, Louisiana: Pelican Publishing Company, 1987.

Garnet, Henry Highland. "Garnet's Call to Rebellion, 1843." *A Documentary History of the Negro People in the United States Volume 1*. Ed. Herbert Aptheker. New York: Carol Publishing Group, 1951. 226-233.

Gerima, Haile. "Spirit of the Dead." *Jump Up and Say! A Collection of Black Storytelling*. Eds. Linda Goss and Clay Goss. New York: Simon and Schuster, 1995.

Glover, Ablade. "Linguist, Staff, Symbolism." Accra, Ghana: Artists Alliance Gallery, 1992.

Goode, Gloria Davis. "Get on Board and Tell Your Story." *Jump Up and Say! A Collection of Black Storytelling*. Eds. Linda Goss and Clay Goss. New York: Simon and Schuster, 1995.

Grayson, Sandra M. "Encoding and Decoding: The *Ifa* Worldview in 'The King Buzzard' and 'Transmigration,'" *CLA Journal*. XLI (December 1997): 161-173.

---. "The Yellow Crane/Agbigbo: A Critique of Black Slaveholders." *CLA Journal*. XL (December 1996): 191-196.

---. "'Spirits of Asona Ancestors Come:' Reading Asante Signs in Haile Gerima's *Sankofa*." *CLA Journal*. XLII (December 1998): 212-227.

---. "A Conversation with Anita Singleton-Prather, Master Storyteller." *Network 2000: In the Spirit of the Harlem Renaissance*. 6.4 (Fall 1999): 1-2.

---. "A Conversation with Fouche Sheppard, Storyteller." *Network 2000: In the Spirit of the Harlem Renaissance*. 6.2 (Spring 1999): 1-3.

---. "A Conversation with Rosalie F. Pazant, President, Gullah Festival of South Carolina, Inc." *Network 2000: In the Spirit of the Harlem Renaissance.* 5.3 (Summer 1998): 1-2.

Hale, Thomas A., ed. *The Epic of Askia Mohammed.* Recounted by Nouhou Malio. Bloomington: Indiana University Press, 1996.

---. "Introduction." *The Epic of Askia Mohammed.* Recounted by Nouhou Malio. Bloomington: Indiana University Press, 1996.

Harper's Weekly. November 27, 1880.

Harris, Trudier. *The Power of the Porch.* Athens: The University of Georgia Press, 1996.

Haviland, Laura S. *A Woman's Life-Work.* Chicago: C.V. Waite and Company, 1887.

Hedges, Inez. "Black Independent Film: An Interview with Haile Gerima." *Socialism and Democracy* 10.1 (Summer 1996): 119-127.

Herskovits, Melville and Frances. *Rebel Destiny.* New York: McGraw-Hill Book Company, 1934.

Herskovits, Melville. *The Myth of the Negro Past.* Boston: Beacon Press, 1990.

---. *Dahomey: An Ancient West African Kingdom Volume II.* Illinois: Northwestern University Press, 1967.

Hill, Phil. "A Remnant of the Past." *The State and the Columbia Record.* November 8, 1964. 2-D.

Hilton, Anne *The Kingdom of Kongo.* Oxford: Clarendon Press, 1985.

Hooks, Bell. *Ain't I a Woman?* Boston, MA: South End Press, 1981.

---. *Black Looks: Race and Representation.* Boston: South End Press, 1992.

---. "Dialogue Between Bell Hooks and Julie Dash, April 26, 1992." *Daughters of the Dust: The Making of An African American Woman's Film.* New York City: The New Press, 1992. 27-67.

Howard, Steve. "A Cinema of Transformation: The Films of Haile Gerima." *Cineaste* 14.1 (1985): 28-29, 39.

Hunter, Janie. "Barney McKay." *Talk that Talk.* Ed. Linda Goss and Marian E. Barnes. New York: Simon and Schuster, 1989.

Hurmence, Belinda, ed. *Before Freedom: When I Can Just Remember.* Winston- Salem: John F. Blair.

---, ed. *We Lived in a Little Cabin.* Winston-Salem: John F. Blair, 1994.

Inikori, J. E. *Forced Migration.* London: Huchinson and Company, 1982.

Irigaray, Luce. *This Sex Which is Not One.* New York: Cornell University Press, 1985.

Jacobs, Harriet. *Incidents in the Life of a Slave Girl*. Ed. Jean Fagan Yellin. Cambridge: Harvard University Press, 1987.

Jeffries, Rosalind. "The Image of Woman in African Cave Art." *Black Women in Antiquity*. Ed. Ivan Van Sertima. New Brunswick: Transaction Publishers, 1992. 98-122.

Johnson-Coleman, Lorraine. *Just Plain Folks*. Boston: Little, Brown and Company, 1998.

Johnson, John William, Thomas Hale, and Stephen Belcher, eds. *The Epic of Almami Samori Toure*. Narrated by Sory Fina Kamara. *Oral Epics from Africa: Voices from a Vast Continent*. Bloomington: Indiana University Press, 1997.

Johnson, Samuel. *The History of the Yorubas*. London: George Routledge and Sons, 1921.

Jones, Howard. "The Peculiar Institution and National Honor: The Case of the *Creole* Slave Revolt." *Civil War History* 21 (1975): 28-50.

Jones-Jackson, Patricia. *When Roots Die: Endangered Traditions on the Sea Islands*. Athens and London: The University of Georgia Press, 1987.

Jones, Jacqueline. *Labor of Love, Labor of Sorrow*. New York: Vintage Books, 1985.

"The King Buzzard." *Tales of the Congaree*. Ed. Robert G. O'Meally. Chapel Hill: University of North Carolina Press, 1987. 120-121.

Koger, Larry. *Black Slaveowners: Free Black Slave Masters in South Carolina, 1790-1860*. North Carolina: McFarland and Company, 1985.

Kuyk, Betty M. "The African Derivation of Black Fraternal Orders in the United States." *Comparative Studies in Society and History* 25: 4 (1983): 559-592.

Lawal, Babatunde. *The Gelede Spectacle and Social Harmony in an African Culture*. Seattle: University of Washington Press, 1996.

Lee, Jarena. *Religious Experience and Journal of Mrs. Jarena Lee, Giving an Account of her Call to Preach the Gospel. Call and Response*. Patricia Liggins Hill, General Editor. Boston: Houghton Mifflin Company, 1998.

Leiding, Harriette Kershaw. *Street Cries of an Old Southern City*. Charleston, South Carolina, 1910.

Leland, Isabella G. "The Vanishing Huckster." *The News and Courier*. September 1, 1957: 1-C.

Lewin, Thomas J. *Asante Before the British: The Prempean Years, 1875-1900*. Lawrence: The Regents Press of Kansas, 1978.

"License Information." New Orleans City Archives Collection. Available at the New Orleans Public Library.

Makinde, Moses Akin. "Immortality of the Soul and the Yoruba Theory of Seven Heavens." *Journal of Cultures and Ideas* 1 (1983): 31- 59.

Marshall, Paule. *Praisesong for the Widow*. New York: E.P. Dutton, 1984.

Mellon, James, ed. *Bullwhip Days: The Slaves Remember*. New York: Avon Books, 1988.

Meyerowitz, Eva L.R. *The Divine Kingship in Ghana and Ancient Egypt*. London: Faber and Faber Limited, 1969.

Monges, Miriam Maat-Ka-Re. *Kush, the Jewel of Nubia*. New Jersey: Africa World Press, 1997.

Morakinyo, Olufemi. "The Yoruba Ayanmo Myth and Mental Health Care in West Africa." *Journal of Cultures and Ideas* 1 (1983): 61-92.

Morrison, Toni. *Beloved*. New York: New American Library, 1987.

Naylor, Gloria. *Mama Day*. New York: Vintage Books, 1993.

Nkansah, M. Y., recorder. "History of Ejisu--Origins and How Ejisu First Became a Member of the Ashanti Confederacy." *Ashanti Stool Histories Volume I*. Compiled by K. Ampom Darkwa and B.C. Obaka. University of Ghana, Legon: Institute of African Studies, 1976. Classification Number 11. 1-3.

Okpewho, Isidore. *African Oral Literature: Backgrounds, Character, and Continuity*. Bloomington: Indiana University Press, 1992.

O'Meally, Robert G. "Introduction." *Tales of the Congaree*. Chapel Hill: University of North Carolina Press, 1987.

Oyewumi, Oyeronke. *The Invention of Women*. Minnesota: University of Minnesota Press, 1997.

Parrish, Lydia. *Slave Songs of the Georgia Sea Islands*. Philadelphia: Folklore Associates, 1965.

Pollitzer, William. "The Relationship of the Gullah-Speaking People of Coastal South Carolina and Georgia to Their African Ancestors." *Historical Methods* 25 (1996): 53-67.

"Report of Governor Hunter on the New York Slave Conspiracy." April 1712. *Crossing the Danger Water*. Ed. Deirdre Mullane. New York: Doubleday, 1993.

Rochefoucault-Liancourt, Duke de la. *Travels Through the United States of North America*. London: R. Phillips, 1799.

Roehl, Marjorie. "Looking Back." *The States*. April 5, 1987.

Sankofa. Videocassette. Written and Directed by Haile Gerima. Mypheduh Films, Inc., 1993. 125 minutes.

Sarpong, Peter. *The Sacred Stools of the Akan*. Tema, Ghana: Ghana Publishing Corporation, 1971.

Sisoko, Fa-Digi. *The Epic of Son-Jara*. Ed. John William Johnson. Bloomington: Indiana University Press, 1992.

Sparkman, Mary A. "Charleston's Street Vendors." *News and Courier*. November 3, 1963.

Starling, Marion Wilson. *The Slave Narrative: Its Place in History*. Howard University Press, 1988.

Stearns, Marshall and Jean. *Jazz Dance: The Story of American Vernacular Dance*. New York: Schirmer Books, 1968.

"A Story of the Underground Railroad." *Douglass' Monthly*. January 1859.

"Street-Vendors and Street Cries." WPA Louisiana Writers' Project. Unpublished Manuscript. Marcus Christian Collection. University of New Orleans Special Collections.

Stuckey, Sterling. *Slave Culture*. New York: Oxford University Press, 1987.

Sweetman, David. *Women Leaders in African History*. New Hampshire: Heinemann, 1984.

Talbot, P. Amaury. *Tribes of the Niger Delta*. New York: Barnes and Noble, 1967.

Thompson, Ben. "Sankofa." *Sight and Sound* 4.7 (July 1994): 53.

Thompson, Robert Farris. *Black Gods and Kings: Yoruba Art at UCLA*. University of California, Los Angeles: Museum and Laboratories of Ethnic Arts and Technologies, 1971.

---. *Flash of the Spirit*. New York: Vintage Books, 1983.

---. *Four Moments of the Sun*. Connecticut: Eastern Press, 1981.

Toledano, Roulhac. *Richard Clague: 1821-1873*. New Orleans Museum of Art, 1974.

"Transmigration." *Tales of the Congaree*. Ed. Robert G. O'Meally. Chapel Hill: University of North Carolina Press, 1987. 60-61.

Tweneboah, Afia. Personal interview. Ejisu, Ghana West Africa. Summer 1998.

Vogel, Susan. "Nigerian Bronze Rings." *The Art of Metal in Africa*. Ed. Marie-Terese Brincard. New York: The African American Institute, 1982. 61-62.

Voices of the Gullah Culture: The Hallelujah Singers. WJWJ-TV Beaufort, South Carolina 1993.

Walker, Juliet E. K. *The History of Black Business in America: Capitalism, Race, Entrepreneurship*. New York: Macmillan Library Reference, 1998.

Wilks, Ivor. *Forests of Gold: Essays on the Akan Kingdom of Asante.* Athens: Ohio University Press, 1993.

Willett, Frank. *African Art.* New York: Thames and Hudson Inc., 1993.

Williams, Shirley Anne "Author's Note." *Dessa Rose.* New York: Berkley Books, 1986.

Wood, Peter H. *Black Majority.* New York: Norton & Company, 1974.

Woolford, Pamela. "Filming Slavery: A Conversation with Haile Gerima." *Transition Conversation* 64 (1994): 90-104.

Yankah, Kwesi. *Speaking for the Chief: Okyeame and the Politics of Akan Royal Oratory.* Bloomington: Indiana University Press, 1995.

"The Yellow Crane." *Tales of the Congaree.* Ed. Robert G. O'Meally. Chapel Hill: University of North Carolina Press, 1987. 53-55.

INDEX

About the Author

Sandra M. Grayson is Associate Professor of English at Bentley College in Massachusetts where she teaches and designs courses in African and African American literature and culture. Her articles on African and African American oral traditions, literature, and film have been published in scholarly journals and collections. She has received numerous research and professional awards including the Avery Research Center for African American History and Culture Research Fellowship and the Faculty Member of the Year Award. She is also the founder and editor of *Network 2000: In the Spirit of the Harlem Renaissance*.